praise for easy does it, mom

"Any parent will find inspiration and encouragement from the beautifully written examples, and will learn many parenting skills to help them be the parents they always wanted to be."

—**Jane Nelsen**, co-author of *Positive Discipline for Parenting in Recovery* and author of *Serenity: Simple Steps for Recovering Peace of Mind, Real Happiness, and Great Relationships*

"*Easy Does It, Mom* is a gem. The format makes the book easy to read for busy parents, and it's filled with helpful, practical, and wise suggestions for positive parenting. Barbara's kindness and experience shine through this useful and touching addition to the parenting literature. A must-read!"

—**Lynn Lott, MA, MFT**, co-author of four books in the *Positive Discipline* series

"As a mom, it is easy to feel that life has supersized itself beyond manageable. Demands tug at you from every direction. *Easy Does It, Mom* is a chance for moms to catch their breath and refocus. It is validation and it is encouragement, which we all need from time to time. Embracing the lessons in *Easy Does It, Mom* will help you to continue to make the world a better place."

—**Mary Rita Schilke Korzan**, author of *When You Thought I Wasn't Looking: A Book of Thanks for Mom*

"In a world rife with anger and lost hope, especially for many parents, *Easy Does It, Mom* is a ray of sunshine. Barbara Joy has provided critical step-by-step help for parents in need of direction. I've already made a list of parents I will give this book to."

—**Earnie Larsen**, author of *The Healer's Way: Bringing Hands-On Compassion to a Love-Starved World*

"I have been Director of Women's Recovery Services for nearly fourteen years and have ... learned from the women and mothers who bravely address their addiction so they can move to the other side with hope and dignity. *Easy Does It, Mom* will give them the tools necessary to be the best possible mothers."

—**Cheryle Stanley,** executive director at Women's Recovery Services

"*Easy Does It, Mom* combines patience, acceptance, honesty, letting go, gratitude, faith, humility, and taking responsibility to help women build strong, healthy families. Joy refers to real-life stories with examples and strategies for moms, including writing activities to put the information in place to better serve the moms and help them gain the knowledge needed to make positive changes in their lives. Joy demonstrates compassion, is straightforward, and is always supportive and nonjudgmental with her work in this field, which also makes her a valuable role model for parenting women."

—**Sharon Youney, PsyD, RAS**

Easy Does It, Mom

Easy Does It, Mom

PARENTING IN RECOVERY

BARBARA JOY

Conari Press

First published in 2009 by Conari Press,
an imprint of Red Wheel/Weiser, LLC
With offices at:
500 Third Street, Suite 230
San Francisco, CA 94107
www.redwheelweiser.com

ISBN: 978-1-57324-412-1
Library of Congress Cataloging-in-Publication Data

Joy, Barbara.
  Easy does it, mom : parenting in recovery / Barbara Joy.
    p. cm.
  ISBN 978-1-57324-412-1 (alk. paper)
  1. Mothers and daughters. 2. Parenting. 3. Recovering addicts. I. Title.
  HQ755.86.J69 2009
  306.874'30874--dc22
                          2008054630

Cover and text design by Tracy Sunrize Johnson
Typeset in Eidetic Modern, Neo, and Serif
Cover/interior images © 2008 Aleksey Telnov/istockphoto

TCP
10 9 8 7 6 5 4 3 2 1

contents

I dedicate these pages to my children,
Scott, Andrea, and Carrie,
for they were the teachers in my classroom.
And to my grandchildren,
Bailey, Keoni, Brooke, and Kylie,
who continue to patiently share their teachings with me daily.

Acknowledgments

One of my consistent messages in this book is about the joy and good feelings that come from giving and receiving gratitude. I also frequently talk about the importance of having a village, not only for our children, but for us as well. There were many within my village who were instrumental in creating *Easy Does It, Mom*.

The gift (actually a miracle) of writing this book came to me in a way that I would never have imagined. Writing has been a passion of mine for many years. I thought I might write a book someday—maybe in my retirement. In January 2008, I took my first "official" writing class from author and artist Mary Anne Radmacher. She saw my potential as a writer. She believed in me enough to introduce me to her publisher, Jan Johnson. My life changed that day.

Mary Anne, thank you for seeing something woven among my words that I had not yet discovered. I am grateful for the generous gift of your time and encouragement, and for the expertise you shared with me. Thank you for guiding (sometimes strongly nudging) me to reach down deep within and find my creativity. Your wit and contagious laughter are a gift in and of themselves. I am honored to have you as a kindred spirit, mentor, and dear friend.

I am grateful to Jan Johnson of Conari Press and to her staff for taking my words, doing their magic, and turning them into this book. I am forever grateful. Jan, I thank you from the bottom of my heart for giving me the opportunity to provide this resource to a group of moms that mean so much to me. Thank you for your time and patience in supporting and guiding me through the process of publishing my first book. I am privileged to have you as my publisher and to be a part of the Conari family.

To Sandy Liddell, Tina Armould, and Grace Meacham, my dear friends who have, over the years, consistently encouraged me to keep writing, I say thank you for your enthusiasm for my written words. You inspired me to keep my fingers on the keyboard.

To Cynara Martin and Joanne LaCasse, my forever friends, and my sister, Patty Pomi, who never wavered in their belief and support while I wrote, I say thank you for always knowing when I needed a phone call or a lunch break. A special thanks to Patty for watching over Mom while I wrote.

To Leslie Cotchett, Andrea Alexander, Grace Meacham, and Mary Gerber, I say thank you for your energy and the hours you spent as my "readers." Your eyes and hearts saw and felt things that made this book even better.

Laura Brown and Andrea Alexander are my computer angels. Thank you for your patience answering my many late-night and early-morning computer questions. Thank you for all of the time you spent on your computers whenever I needed your help. I cannot even imagine what I would have done without the two of you.

Thank you to the many moms in recovery, especially those that I have learned so much from at Women's Recovery Services. We have been students and teachers to one another. It is a gift to be a part of your lives and your journeys as moms. You are women of tremendous strength, courage, and perseverance. Thank you for aspiring to be the best moms you can be. I know you will be supportive and encouraging for other moms in recovery.

A special thank you to the children of the moms in recovery who opened their hearts and shared their true thoughts and experiences with me. I have learned many important lessons from you, as will every mom who reads this book. Your contributions within these pages are full of insight and wisdom.

I am grateful to Executive Director Cheryle Stanley, and to the staff at Women's Recovery Services. Thank you Cheryle, Tina, Laura, and Mary for helping me more fully understand addiction and recovery. I appreciate your openness and willingness to share your knowledge and expertise with me.

To Mel Newman, my friend in South Africa, I say thank you for gifting me with a journal when I first arrived in your country and another when I left, and for telling me to keep writing every day. My time with you changed my life and inspired me to write in new ways.

To my three children and their partners, Scott and Kathleen Osborn, Andrea and Zack Alexander, and Carrie Osborn—thank you for your unconditional love, support, and continued interest in the creation of this book. You called when I needed an encouraging voice or a good laugh, and remained silent when I needed to write. I also thank you for allowing me to share some of the challenges and joys we experienced during your childhood. I am honored beyond words to be your mom.

A special thank you to my "Board of Directors"—my four grandchildren, Bailey, Keoni, Brooke, and Kylie. Without you I might have forgotten to take time to laugh and play during this process. You are my greatest inspiration and joy.

Last, but by no means least, thanks to my forever faithful and unconditional four-legged friend, Edgrrr B. Joyful, age fourteen, who patiently lay on my piles of papers night after night as I created this book.

introduction

This book is for you. I've written it because I know you, like every mom, want to do the very best job raising your children that you can. Being a mom can be overwhelming and exhausting, with few expressions of gratitude coming to you for all of your hard work. I can tell you this because I am a mom of three now-grown children. In spite of the many peaks and valleys (sometimes cliffs and pits!), all three of them grew up to be loving, responsible, self-reliant adults. Being a mom has been the most challenging, as well as the most rewarding, chapter of my life. It is my greatest success. I wish the very same for you and your children.

You and I have things in common. We are moms. Have you ever noticed how moms have an understanding of one another that others don't share? We know how hard it can be. We know how we hurt when they hurt. How we miss them when they are not with us. We know how much we wish they would just behave when they are with us! Many times, as moms, we feel alone and isolated. We wonder if we are the only moms feeling out of control and helpless—wanting to be good moms and not knowing what to do.

This book will help you to become the best mom you can be. Within these pages, you will discover many effective tools that you can begin using today with your children. You will most likely be pleasantly surprised to find that, as you begin to parent in a more positive way, your children will respond in the same way.

For the past twenty-five years, I have worked with parents and children in many arenas—teaching, nursing, advocating, coaching, and consulting. I am passionate about helping parents acquire positive parenting tools that can help them raise children who are happy and healthy, with good self-esteem. It is equally important for you to build your confidence as a mom and be proud of how you parent. While I am not a mom in recovery, I have worked with many moms over the years who have been. Moms in recovery and their children have generously shared with me their true experiences. You'll find them within the pages of this book. The names have been changed to respect their anonymity.

Anyone who is involved in a child's life will benefit from this book. The child will also benefit, because the more that the important people in his life model "respectful parenting," the better for the child. These important people include:

Moms in recovery	Teachers
Family members	Counselors and therapists
Friends, even if they don't have children	Human resource professionals
	Physicians
Dads in recovery	Pediatricians
Day-care providers	

As a way of supporting you in your reading, I've included three sections at the end of every chapter. The first one is a journaling activity. I will give you some suggestions about things you may want to spend a little time thinking about and writing down.

Journaling may be new to some of you. When you journal, there is no right or wrong. It is merely a way for you to process your thoughts, feelings, ideas, and experiences. Many times, writing something down helps you let go. Sometimes you may find yourself feeling better or even getting clarity on a situation.

Your journal can be anything from an actual hardbound journal, to a notebook, to a piece of paper you happen to have with you when you want to write. The journal is only for you, unless you choose to share it with someone. Find a place where it will be safe, so that you will have the freedom to write whatever you need to write whenever you need to write it. You can also explain to your family that it contains your personal thoughts and that no one else is to read it. This is one way to teach your children about respecting each other's privacy. Many children, some as young as age eight, enjoy journaling. What a wonderful way for your children to sort through some of their feelings.

The second section at the end of each chapter is called Gems for Your Pocket. These are short phrases or sentences that highlight some of the key points in the chapter. I call them gems because I think of them as tiny nuggets, full of wisdom, that you can carry with you throughout your day.

The third section is Affirmations. Affirmations are short, simple, positive statements to say, think, and feel about yourself. I encourage you to write them at least twice a day. Say them out loud while looking in your mirror. Go ahead. Be brave. You can do it, even if you feel silly. Carry them with you. Put them in a spot where you will see them during your day—in your binder, on your dashboard, on the fridge. Be creative and add some of your own. Include them in your daily prayer time. How about making a section in your journal for affirmations?

One recurring theme in this book is the importance of giving your child encouragement. You need and deserve it too. This book is filled with inspiration and encouragement for you, and at the end of the book, there are Recommended Readings that give you more information on many topics we will talk about here.

You are a woman of courage and strength. I acknowledge you for remaining committed to your recovery. It is the greatest gift you can give your children.

I wish for you continued determination and healing, as you move forward, one step at a time, to be the very best mom you can be.

who do you want to be?

> Parenting is a two way street.
> As you take them by the hand,
> they will take you by the heart.
>
> —*Judy Ford*

Every mom wants to be the best mom she can be. I understand that you may be struggling, not only with guilt and shame from your past, but now also because you are a woman in recovery and a mom at the same time. A mom that wants her children to grow up to love, trust, and respect her. A mom who will be there for her children during the good and not-so-good times. Teaching your child to one day become a loving and responsible adult is important. You, like every mom, want to succeed. Every day you remain in your recovery, you are succeeding.

Every child wants to have a happy and safe childhood. All children want to have moms they trust and know will protect and provide for them. They want stability, consistency, and structure in their lives. Another word for structure is routine. *Routine is more than a schedule. It's a rhythm.*

Some days seem to flow smoothly. Other days are full of chaos and confusion. *When children have a routine, they feel more safe and secure. When they feel more safe and secure, there is less need to act out.* Parents often ask why their children do well at school, but not at home. Many times, this is because children know the routine at school. They know what to expect in their day. If you want support in creating a routine for your family, take a look at *Positive Discipline for Parenting in Recovery* by Jane Nelsen, Riki Intner, and Lynn Lott. They lay out many helpful daily routines.

In addition to routine, what children most want are moms who are *present* with them on a regular basis. Being present is when you stop what you are doing, or when you plan for times in the day during which you genuinely are paying attention to your child. Children know that this is their special time with you. They feel important, that they matter in your life.

Looking Back so You Can Move Forward

Some of you had parents who were very strict and used punishments as discipline—restrictions, hitting, threats, yelling, grounding, and physical, emotional, or verbal abuse. This is called an authoritarian style of discipline.

Others were raised by permissive parents—parents who did not provide rules or boundaries. They were inconsistent and passive. Bribing and pleading were frequent discipline tools. The child had the power and was in charge. It may appear that children want to be in charge. They don't. They want to be kids—to play and have fun. They want parents who will help them learn to make good choices.

It's common that one parent is authoritarian and the other permissive. Sometimes, this occurs because the parents think they are balancing each other out. If one parent is too strict, the other may tend to be easy on the kids, thinking this will compensate for the other's strictness, and vice versa. Children with parents like this have to figure out how to behave, depending on which parent is with them at any given moment. When the permissive parent is there, no one is in charge unless they take on that role. When the authoritarian parent is there, they are most likely anxious and fearful, not knowing what is going to happen next.

A young mom, Liz, shared this with me. "My father was an alcoholic and very authoritarian when he did parent me. I grew up in uncertainty because I never knew what 'mood' my father would be in when he came home. The more he drank, the meaner he got. Sometimes, he came in the door yelling at us kids and cursing my mother. Other times, he beat us and locked us in our rooms. My mother was the submissive parent, most likely out of fear of my dad. I think she would take anything he said or did in order to protect us kids. It was very scary. I lost respect for both of them and left home at seventeen."

While children are adaptable and resilient, this kind of parenting causes confusion and stress. Many times, it leads to manipulation and playing parents against each other. This benefits no one in the family. Children are not born manipulative. It is a learned behavior that they develop from the important adults in their lives. Sometimes, it is the only way that they know how to survive.

Presents or Presence

Presence or presents? What do your children really want? There is no doubt. They not only want, *they need* your presence. You are the gift. Being present with your child does not have to involve money, treats, or toys. It involves a mom who can simply be with her child. Maybe it's taking a walk, reading a book, sitting quietly and just talking, or doing a creative project together. Maybe it's pulling weeds, planting a garden, folding clothes. The "what" does not much matter. What matters is that you are concentrating on your child during this time. The TV, phone, computer, reading the newspaper, talking with a friend, or whatever else may distract you, is off-limits for the time being. If you can find ways to slow down during your busy days and give your children some genuinely present time, that gift will far outweigh anything that you can buy them. It is a lasting gift that will be cherished by you both. Sometimes, we may forget or do not fully realize just what a gift we are in our children's lives. *Give them the gift of your presence.*

Many moms say this feels weird and uncomfortable. You may not have experienced anyone in your life being present with you. So how can you do this with your child? Start simple. A few minutes at a time. Sometimes it's helpful to think of something that you both enjoy and do that together. Before long, you will begin to see your child in a new and wonderful way—a child full of love, and wanting to be an important part of your life.

Very young children need short, but frequent, times throughout the day for you to connect with them. As children get older, although it is wonderful to do, sometimes it's not realistic to find time daily. In that case, you can let them know that you want to spend some special time with just them, and that you will be able to do something together on the coming weekend.

The next time your child is acting out, ask yourself, "When was the last time I gave him (or her) some of my undivided attention?" Often, if, instead of battling with them over and over, you just stop what you are doing and spend a little time, without interruption, the day improves for you both.

Let's say a good friend of yours comes for a visit. She has a nicely wrapped gift for you. Would you rather have the wrapped gift or thirty minutes to sit down and have a cup of coffee and talk? When I ask moms this question, I get the same answer. The coffee and talk. It is far richer and longer-lasting than a material gift. Children are the same way. You may think that they would choose the new video game over spending time with you. And they may at first. But once they know that they can actually have you and your undivided attention, that is what they will choose. *Children crave their mom's presence.*

Your presence is a lasting gift that fills the heart, builds self-esteem, and cements the relationship between you and your child. We'll be talking more about building healthy self-esteem in chapter 6.

when you know better, you do better

When you became a mom, you most likely found yourself parenting in a way very similar to the way you were parented. *We do what we know, and when we know better, we do better.*

Have you ever noticed your face in the mirror when you were angry and thought, "Yikes, I look just like my mother did when she was mad at me?" Or have you heard your mother's exact words and tone coming out of your own mouth when you were frustrated with your child? Most of us have, more than once. These are things we hoped we'd never do to our own children.

At a very young age, we take the experiences of how we are treated and what we are told about ourselves deep within us. Believing them to be true, most of us pass on those behaviors and beliefs to our own children, until we learn new, more positive ways of parenting and change our beliefs about ourselves. A small number of parents who were more severely abused will, many times, swing to the exact opposite of how they were raised.

Beverly said, "I was raised by a permissive parent. There was absolutely no structure or organization. No rules, limits, consequences. She wasn't home often, but when she was, nothing was any different. My life was always full of chaos and confusion. When I had my first child, I was determined never to treat him like that. I became very strict. There were consequences for almost everything. Actually, they were punishments. Finally, after my third child was born, I took a parenting class. I learned that there's a balance between being permissive like my own mom had been and being a tyrant like I had been. I am working on finding effective ways to parent. My children seem to be acting out less. I try not to beat myself up because it took me so long. But it sure is easier this way."

Fortunately, today there is support and education for parents to learn ways of parenting that are more effective than punishment. You can teach and guide your children to become responsible and loving. The good news is that, once parents begin to make positive changes in their parenting style, they most likely will soon see improvement in their children's behavior and attitude.

punishment versus Discipline

Discipline and punishment are not the same thing. When used correctly, punishment is a very small part of discipline. Punishment usually has something aggressive and/or punitive in it. Discipline does not.

Parents have said to me more than once, "Punishment works. When I spank them, they straighten up." This may appear to be true. Children may straighten up in that moment, but are they learning anything from the spanking? I believe what they are learning is that they must be pretty bad kids, because their parents had to hit them. They are learning to behave out of fear, not learning to behave because it's the right thing to do.

Every time a child is spanked, his or her self-esteem goes down. Positive discipline leads to raising children who have healthy self-esteem. Aggression teaches aggression. If moms hit when they are frustrated, children learn to hit when they are frustrated. If moms talk respectfully and listen to their children, their children will learn to do the same.

Discipline includes all those things we, as parents, do to teach our children how to make better decisions. Discipline teaches them to become responsible, to think for themselves, to make better choices. Many parents think of discipline as punishment. Below are some differences that can help you to understand how they are different.

DISCIPLINE	PUNISHMENT
Emphasizes what the child *can* do	Emphasizes what the child *cannot* do
Is a continuous process	Is a one-time occurrence
Models behavior for the child	Insists on obedience
Is positive	Is negative
Helps a child to think for him or herself	Thinks for the child
Builds up self-esteem	Breaks down self-esteem

Implementing new discipline tools is no easy undertaking. It is a one-new-tool and one-step-at-a-time process. As the psychologist Abraham Maslow so famously said back in the 1960s, "If the only tool you have is a hammer, then every problem is a nail." For example, let's say that all you know how to do is yell. When your children misbehave in any way, you yell—whether you are trying to make sure they stop at the stop sign, or they have just spilled their milk, or they are fighting with their brother, you yell. Try and save the yelling voice for when something is really important, especially in regard to their safety. If you yell all of the time, they won't be listening when you need them to stop at the stop sign. They will have tuned you out because yelling is what you always do. You need to have different tools for different situations with your children.

Learning new and effective ways to parent is like being in another country and having to learn the language. The words are not familiar. You don't know how to make your requests understood. It takes time and practice. Each positive change you make will help you break the cycle of how you were parented. You and your child will experience parenting in a more positive way.

Moms frequently ask if it's too late for them and their children to build a healthy relationship. My answer is: No, it's never too late. You have already taken a huge step toward the healing of the relationship by remaining in recovery.

Especially with adolescents, teens, and grown children, the process may take longer than you would like. I encourage you to give them time and space. We all come to healing and forgiveness in our time and in our own way. Pray for patience and understanding at these times. *Your children need to see the changes in you rather than hear more words.* Show them that they can trust you, that you are there for them. Accept them exactly as they are. With time, they will see that you are strong in your recovery.

The Qualities of a Mom

I once asked a group of moms what I thought was a simple question: "What is a mom?" The room quieted. The question was not easy. For some, the question brought immediate grief and regret. I decided to break it down: "What are the qualities of a mom?"

These amazing women knew the qualities of what a mom could be. Before we knew it, we had a whole board full of words describing mom:

Is kind	Helps with homework
Keeps them safe	Comes home right after work
Listens	Is consistent, patient, fun
Has a job, money	Makes dinner
Talks with her children respectfully	And, most of all, is clean and sober.

We moved on to talk about their own childhoods. Which of these traits did their mothers have? The room once again became silent. This was an uncomfortable place for them to go. Some were holding back the tears. One was muttering sarcastic remarks under her breath. One got up and went to the bathroom. Another stood up and swore in frustration.

With a little encouragement, these brave women began to share their stories. Tears flowed. Voices went from softly getting the words out, to anger that temporarily covered up the wounds. The more they shared, the more they were able to add to the list of qualities we had begun just minutes ago:

Gives structure, consistency, and routine

Doesn't yell

Makes floor time

Plays at the park

Reads a bedtime story every night

Our picture of the moms they wanted to be was building. They didn't fully realize it, but they were already well on their way to being the moms they wanted to be. There is no perfect mom! And yet, with every positive step a mom takes practicing effective parenting, she is one step closer to creating the relationship she wants with her children. And to becoming the mom she wants to be.

Marie, a mom of two, said, "A mom is someone who is nurturing, loving, and accepting, and raises her children to be strong, independent adults one day. She's affectionate, encouraging, and fun-loving, but serious when it's appropriate." Her faced changed. "It sounds so good. But is anyone really like that?"

Sue, mom of five, chimed in. "A mom is someone that my children are proud of. They want me to be involved at their school. They are not ashamed of me anymore. They know they can count on me to care for them and not embarrass them. Marie, I know what you mean. I keep remembering that there is no such thing as a perfect mom—that every positive change makes a difference. I try to focus on what I am doing right, not on when I foul up."

Sue brought up a great point. Another excellent positive discipline tool is to *catch them being good.* We are experts at catching our children when they do things we don't want them to do. But how often do we remember to notice the good and simply acknowledge it?

For example, when you have a car full of kids and they all happen to be getting along and not yelling, all you need to say is, "Thank you for your cooperation when we were in the car. I appreciate it." For most of us, when someone says "thank you," it makes us want to repeat that same behavior. Children are no different. It may not always seem so, but they do want to please you and have your approval. We will be talking more about acknowledgment in chapter 8. Meanwhile, as Tom Peters says, "Celebrate what you want to see more of." Now we come to *real* experts—the children. When asked to describe what a mom is, Alyssa, Marie's eight-year-old daughter, said, "My mom is loving, caring, thoughtful, helps me, worries about me sometimes, takes me places, checks in with me, and cuddles. She is nice, patient, usually in a good mood, funny, sometimes a little dorky, listens to me, and is honest with me."

Sue's fifteen-year-old daughter, Becca, added, "My mom listens to me more than she talks at me. She trusts me until I foul up. When I do, she doesn't shame or punish me. She does help me so next time I will make a better choice. Sometimes, I have to show her all over again that she can trust me. It frustrates me that she won't just believe me right away. She doesn't yell or nag often. When she's mad, she takes a 'cooling off time.' We all appreciate that."

Sue's five-year-old daughter, Halle, said, "My mom meets me at the bus every day with my snack in her pocket. She reads two books to me every night, makes good dinners, and doesn't leave me home alone anymore. That's the best part."

understanding chiLdren

I learned the hard way that there are three fundamental areas of parenting that a mom needs to understand:

What is your style of discipline?

What is your child's temperament? What is yours?

What developmental stage is your child in?

If you don't understand these aspects of you and your child, it can be even more challenging to parent in a way that works well for you both.

I like to be open and honest about my mistakes as a mom in the hope that some other mom and her children will benefit. It took me nearly four years to figure out what temperament was all about. It wasn't anything that the pediatrician or anyone else talked about.

Our first son was what I call my "Gerber" baby—easygoing, happy, very social and adaptable. For him, the more excitement and people around, the better. As young parents, we thought that he was like this because we were such good parents, and so we decided to have another baby. Ha!

I imagine you can guess what I am about to say. Two and a half years later, our daughter was born. She arrived screaming and pretty much continued that way until her fourth birthday. She was my "Velcro baby." She liked being stuck to me as much as she could. She was happiest when it was only she and I. She preferred to hang back, peering from behind my skirt, whenever we went into any kind of a social situation.

So, here I am, the mom of two—one happiest when we are on the go and surrounded by people; the other happiest when she is quietly clinging to me, observing what's going on. She threw tantrums nearly every day of her first four years.

I could not figure out what I was doing wrong. Why was she so unhappy much of the time? Why couldn't she be happy like her brother? Most of the time, I didn't even know what had set her off. My confidence as a mom diminished. I was parenting her the very same way that I was parenting her brother. But it wasn't working at all.

Just before her fourth birthday, I took a parenting class, "Understanding Your Child's Temperament." At last I understood why she was so unhappy. Being the extrovert that I am, like my son, I mistakenly "assumed" that my daughter would be the same way. Even though she kept showing me she wasn't, I somehow missed the signs. She is as much an introvert as her brother is an extrovert. Neither one is right or wrong. Good or bad. I just needed to learn to parent her somewhat differently than my son.

I hope this scenario will show you what I mean. When my son sees a swimming pool, he immediately dives in, clothes and all. When my daughter sees the same pool, she observes the situation and, in her own time, puts on her suit and takes a swim. They both end up in the water. They just get there in their own time and their own way.

Once I began parenting my daughter for who she truly is, she almost immediately became a happy and contented little girl. Believe it or not, the tantrums stopped within days once I figured out how to parent her more appropriately. I finally understood that she is happier being a quiet observer than she is when she has to be out in the middle of a crowd of people. She enjoys small groups rather than big ones. I learned not to overwhelm her with my expectations. She needed time to go from one task to another. This is called *transitioning*. Many children, and some adults too, need time to transition from one activity to the next. If my daughter was playing in her room and I, all of a sudden, appeared and said, "We gotta go now. Get your coat," she fell apart. I learned to go in and say, "Andrea, I'm setting the timer. It's almost time to leave for school. When the timer rings, it's time to go." This way, she had some time to get ready for the change in her own way. I could not believe how smooth the transition went. As I made a simple change in my parenting, she made a change in her behavior.

what is temperament?

In the 1950s, Chess, Thomas, and Burch began longitudinal studies that identified nine personality traits that combine to make up an individual's personal style. These traits are inherited and then influenced by a child's environment.

Genetically, we are born into this world with a natural way of interacting with people, places, and things. This is our temperament.

As we grow, depending on how we are raised, what is going on in our environment, and what we experience, our personalities form and grow. Personality is a combination of our temperaments and life experiences.

The nine traits identified in the study are neutral, although they are often seen as positive or negative in a child. As moms, we need to help our children accept themselves for exactly who they are. We also need to accept them for exactly who they are.

It's important to know that the traits that may be most challenging for you to deal with now may become some of your children's greatest attributes when they are grown. For example, moms have often said to me, "He is so stubborn. I can't stand it." Rather than labeling children as stubborn, I advise parents to think of them as strong-willed. Children can be very determined. I do understand that it is sometimes a challenge to deal with a determined child. However, in order for most of us to do well in this world, it takes a lot of determination. "Stubborn" children will most likely grow up to be very determined adults who will set goals and accomplish them thanks to this part of their natural temperament.

When I was a child, my parents frequently told me to calm down, not to be so loud, to be more like my sister. She was a much quieter child and much more easygoing than I. I was full of exuberance. If I was happy, I was very happy. If I was sad, I was very sad. No matter what I was feeling, it was intensified. Anyone who happened to be in my presence knew exactly how I was feeling. I exhausted my mother much of the time. She was not an intense person at all. She didn't know what to do with me. I actually liked being that way, until about age five. I remember hearing negative comments about me pass between her and my older brother—as though being too happy were a bad thing. Fortunately, I was strong-willed enough not to change my level of intensity. Whatever I felt, I felt it to the max. Today, I imagine anyone who knows me well would say I am intense. I am glad to be. I like feeling whatever I am experiencing to the fullest. I am passionate about the things that are important in my life. It's my strong feelings about being a mom and supporting other moms that led me to write this book.

As you read through these nine temperament traits, think of both your own temperament and your child's:

1. **Approach/withdrawal:** What is your initial response to new persons or situations?

2. **Adaptability:** How easily do you or your child adapt to change?

3. **Intensity:** How strongly do you react?

4. **Activity level:** How much movement do you or your child need during the day and night?

5. **Regularity:** How consistent is your daily pattern of biological functions (eating, sleeping, elimination)?

6. **Sensory threshold:** What is your response to sound, light, touch, pain?

7. **Mood:** Is your mood usually positive or negative? Are you and your child easily soothed when you are upset?

8. **Distractability:** Do you have a long or short attention span? Are you easily distracted or very focused?

9. **Persistence:** Are you easily frustrated? Are you strong-willed and don't like to give up on anything?

when Temperaments cLash

It is helpful to be clear about your own temperament. You can then target the areas where you may have conflict with your child due to a clash of temperaments. Sometimes, you clash because you share a temperament trait with your child—for example, if you are both strong-willed. On the other hand, if you are a very focused person and your child tends to be distracted easily, you may be frustrated until you understand that there is no right or wrong here—that you just have opposing ways when it comes to concentration and focus. Once you are both aware and accepting of each other as you are, parenting your child will most likely go more smoothly.

Sometimes, parents naturally find it easier to deal with one child than with another. This is not about love. It's most likely about temperament. Your temperament may be more conducive to dealing with one child than with the other. It is your job to find ways to parent each child in a way that will be most effective for you both.

It is also important to understand your child's developmental stage. Parents often have unrealistic expectations of their children. Challenges and frustrations arise for both child and parent.

For example, you have a two-year-old, and a second baby comes along. Many times, a mom will unconsciously think, "Now that I have an infant, you (the two-year-old) need to be grown up." You may tend your first child as if he or she were older and more capable, rather than remembering that a mere twenty-four months separate the children and your firstborn still needs to be parented as a two-year-old.

It can also go the other way. As children move into adolescence, they need and want to become more independent. If you hold on to them too tightly and treat them "like babies," there will most likely be conflict between you. They will also be missing out on some important developmental steps that are age-appropriate.

Louise Bates Ames, from the Gesell Institute of Human Development, has written a series of books that starts with *Your One-Year-Old* and goes up to *Your Ten- to Fourteen-Year-Old.* You can find them in any library or bookstore. I encourage parents to get the books that are appropriate to their children's ages and read them the month of their birthday, and again six months later. This is because children develop so rapidly.

Understanding what your children may be experiencing developmentally can often ease concerns and worries. Just knowing that some of what they are doing is "normal" can decrease your stress.

Discipline styles

There are three styles of parental discipline. At the beginning of this chapter, we talked about the authoritarian and permissive parenting styles. The third is called the democratic parenting style.

When I asked the women in a workshop what word they would use to describe the democratic style, they said, "leader, guide, loving teacher." Can you imagine what it would have been like to have had a mom who was truly a loving teacher, guiding you as you grew up? I asked them, "What qualities would this parent have?"

Janice, mom of twelve-year-old Jacob, said, "My dad was very strict, authoritarian. I think my mom was democratic. She was easy to talk to when my dad wasn't around. She didn't yell much. She listened to us kids. The more she listened, the more I talked. She set limits and rules for us. My mom was always fair. She didn't spoil us. She treated us respectfully and, in return, we treated her that way. It was very different with our dad. He yelled and we yelled back. He slammed doors and we slammed doors. I don't see much of him today. I know I am blessed to have had the mom I did. I hope I am following many of her ways with Jacob."

Before we continued our discussion, I asked the moms which style they most identified with. Of the thirty present, seventeen said authoritarian, eleven said permissive, and two said democratic. I then asked them what they wanted to be a year from now. Two said authoritarian and twenty-eight said democratic. We were on our way. What parts of your parenting do you want to keep? What parts do you want to release?

Patty, mother of four and grandmother of five, said, "I've made many mistakes, but now that I am clean and sober, I do it differently. I try to talk to my kids without raising my voice. I think that keeping a *neutral tone* is the most helpful positive discipline tool. When I manage not to yell, they respond so much better. But, I must say, it isn't easy. I feel much better about myself when I remember not to yell."

Amanda, mother of two teens, said, "I'm learning to talk less. My daughters appreciate it. They don't call me a nag or just walk off with an attitude. We try to sit down for dinner at least three or four times a week. Sometimes, I insist on it. We are all so busy that, at least during these times, we have the opportunity to talk about our week."

"I didn't have my children with me for nearly six years. I don't take being a mom for granted. I am privileged and blessed to get a second chance. I want to be a mom my daughters are proud of." Karen added, "I am learning how to set clear and age-appropriate limits for them. They are still testing me. Most of the time, I tell them what the consequences will be if they don't abide by the limits. If they don't, I follow through. That's the hardest part for me. *Being consistent and following through is so important.*"

Lisa, mom of seven-year-old twins, said, "I want to quit threatening and bribing, but I don't know what else to do. I get desperate. They are old enough to know that I won't follow through. They just blow me off. It scares me to think how it will be when they become teenagers if I don't make some changes now."

Andrea, mom of three and a newborn added, "I neglected my kids before recovery, and they are no longer with me. I want to bond with this baby. I need to hold her more, talk to her even though it's hard for me. I know it's important. I feel guilty that I wasn't there for my first three children. I want her to know that I am her mom."

Jennifer, mom of four, piped in, "Someone recently told me that I can't parent from the couch. I got it! I'm lazy. *Lazy is not a word that describes a mom.* I've always been permissive. Now I know I need to turn off the TV and be more involved with my kids. When they make me mad, I need to find other ways to deal with it other than slapping them. First, I need to get my own anger under control. Once I do that and they have also cooled off, then we can begin to talk together about finding a solution. I know that they want me to have reasonable rules for them and to follow through on what I say. I know that, as I make some changes and show more effort, they will be more cooperative and respectful. My first step is get off the couch even when I don't want to!"

BuiLding a ReLationship for the Future

When your child is grown and comes home for a visit, what do you want your relationship to be like?

Suzanne, mom of nineteen- and twenty-one-year-olds, volunteered, "I want them to come visit because they want to. Even though they are independent and living on their own, they still feel as if they are home. It's a place of good memories. I want them to be glad to see me and vice versa."

Amanda said, "I want to be a sounding board for my kids. I want to be able to listen to them, without judgment or advising. I want to offer them encouragement and remind them how much I believe in them, just as they are."

Tonja added, "I want everything that Suzanne and Amanda said. I also want to continue with the traditions that we created when they were young. When they have children, I hope we will be a close family and support one another."

Frannie, mom of nineteen-year-old Beverly, took a piece of paper out of her bag. "My daughter wrote me a note, in the form of a prayer, after her last visit." She then read it to the group.

> Thank you for giving my mom and me this day together. I am grateful to be a part of her life and I know she is grateful to be a part of mine. We are loving and open, and trust one another. Help us always to remember to show love and gratitude for all that we have. Most of all, thank you for giving my mom the strength and courage to remain in her recovery for all these years.

With tears in her eyes, Frannie said, "What more could I ask for?"

Lynn, mom and grandmother, said, "My three grandsons and I often go hiking together. Recently, we hiked up to the top of a mountain we had always wanted to climb. Everyone fell to the ground when we finally arrived, hot and tired. I pulled out a juice box and a small apple for each of us. I've learned it's important to *plan ahead* when you're the mom or the nana. When it was time, we headed back down the hill. While the two younger ones were galloping down the hillside, my oldest grandson, who had been quiet all morning, was lagging behind. I slowed my pace and joined him. We walked in silence. After a few minutes, he said, 'Nana, I didn't make the baseball team. Are you disappointed in me? I really did try hard, but I am not good enough.' I paused, took his hand, and acknowledged his disappointment, reassuring him that I would never be ashamed of him. I knew he had done his best. 'Maybe baseball isn't one of your sports, but we know soccer sure is.' He lit up. He felt better. Smiling, he began running, trying to catch his two brothers."

"I wish I had a nana like that," interjected Louisa. Many nodded in agreement.

Lynn had shared her experience and had also given several helpful tools:

She had planned ahead with a simple snack. Can you imagine how the boys might have begun behaving if there had not been something to rejuvenate them from the hike?

She gave her grandson time and space. Lynn made herself available if he chose to talk about what was bothering him.

She acknowledged his disappointment. Pointing out one of his other strengths was also helpful.

Children believe what they are told about themselves. If they are told they are dumb, they believe it. Soon, they may be struggling in school, because they have taken on the belief that they are dumb. So why should they try?

The opposite is also true. If children are raised being told that you believe in them, that they can accomplish anything they set their minds to, they will likely have self-confidence, set goals, and work toward achieving them.

A single word can be life-changing. Pay attention to the words you use. What messages are you sending? What would you rather hear?

"I cannot believe you did something so stupid," OR
"I trust you will do the right thing."

"You'll never stay in recovery," OR
"You are strong in your recovery."

"You hang out with such losers," OR
"I trust you to choose your friends wisely."

Our subconscious takes us literally. It does not know when we are being sarcastic, funny, positive, or negative. It does not know the difference between reality and any other thoughts or images we have. In other words: *What we continually think and speak about eventually shows up in our lives.* Words and thoughts are very powerful. Pay attention to them.

My Acknowledgment for You

I acknowledge you for finishing the first chapter of this book! This is a success! Give yourself a pat on the back! Start keeping a list of your little and big successes. Sometimes, seeing something in black and white is helpful. It's important not to overlook even the smallest victories. You are working so hard. Whether it's that you arrived at work on time, refrained from swatting your child, did the dishes, took a walk, made those two phone calls you've been needing to make, or used a neutral tone even though you felt like screaming, it's all success.

JOURNALING ACTIVITY

1. With what discipline style do you most identify? Why?

2. How would you describe your child's temperament? Is it different from or similar to yours?

3. List at least five qualities you have as a mom that you feel good about.

4. Take each quality and write an example of how that quality assists you in your parenting.

5. Presence or presents. Which one do you currently give to your children? How does it benefit them?

6. Your children want your presence. Write some of the ways that you give it to them.

7. What positive discipline tools did you discover in this chapter? How can you begin using them with your child?

8. What's the best thing about being a mom? What's the hardest thing?

GEMS FOR YOUR POCKET

Continue to let go of the past. Live in this day.

Be present with your child every day. Start with ten to fifteen minutes and build up.

Talk less. Listen more.

Watch for opportunities to catch your child being good. Acknowledge those times.

Children want and need structure. When they have this, they feel more safe and secure. When they feel safe and secure, there is less need to act out.

Your child wants your presence. It's far more meaningful and lasting than a present.

Be kind and gentle to yourself. Being a mom is no easy task.

There is no such thing as a perfect mom. Be the best you can be.

Enjoy the journey.

Remind yourself throughout the day to use a neutral tone.

Be consistent.

AFFIRMATIONS

I am present with my child every day.

I am open to receive new and positive ways to parent my children.

I am a loving guide to my children. They can count on me.

I encourage those around me as much as I can.

I accept my children exactly as they are.

I accept myself exactly as I am.

I am grateful for all that I have.

I am strong in my recovery.

I am enough.

vaLues, Traditions, and RituaLs

If we don't stand up for children, then we don't stand for much.

—Marian Wright Edelman

When I finally got my children raised, I was both relieved and proud. Relieved because being a mom of three is the most challenging thing I've ever done. It is also the accomplishment that I am most proud of. In spite of the ups and downs and mistakes along the way, all three of them are now loving, responsible adults. What more could any mom want? I've never met a mom who didn't want to raise her children to be loving, responsible individuals with healthy self-esteem. Every mom wants to succeed.

Having healthy values, not only for yourself, but for your children, is important. I imagine you want to instill honesty, responsibility, faith, patience, kindness, forgiveness, acceptance, humor, and compassion in your children. You may have more that you want to add to the list.

Some of you were raised with family traditions and rituals. Others were not. Now you can begin creating traditions and rituals that will be meaningful for your family. If you don't know what you want to do, talk with your children. They may have some great ideas. Or talk with friends and see what they do to bring traditions into their families.

Every mom wants to create a better life for her children than she may have had. You have probably seen the bumper sticker that reads, "It's never too late to have a happy childhood." What you didn't get to experience in your own childhood, you can now experience with your children as you create meaningful traditions.

Children want to have happy lives. They want to be safe and well taken care of. Becoming loving, healthy, independent, responsible adults one day is important. Pleasing you and having your approval matters to them. They want to learn right from wrong. They want to grow up having wonderful traditions and rituals. It will be a meaningful and lasting gift for them. They want to have a close and supportive family.

They want to feel good about themselves just as they are—to feel accepted by you and those around them. Every child wants to have a happy childhood.

Looking Back so you can Move Forward

What were your parents' values? I've asked many moms this question and, while there is a wide range of answers, there are also similarities between them.

About one in ten include these in their list: honesty, no stealing, taking care of children, family, kindness, not swearing, doing what you say, not talking back, showing respect for others, a steady job, good hygiene, table manners, and a good education.

The other nine out of ten said their parents valued alcohol, drugs, marijuana, sex, gambling, fighting, abuse, and using anyone they could to get what they wanted.

Now that you are the mom, you can choose which values you want to bring into your family and which ones to discard. I asked a group of moms to list their values and traditions. Here's what they came up with:

Taking care of and providing
for their children

Love

Honesty

Being trustworthy

Education

Family

Obeying the law

Relationships

Happiness

Respect of self and others

Trust

Friends

Maintaining sobriety

Having a nice home

Being a good mother

Being responsible

Patience

Manners

Keeping a good job

Next, we talked about the values that they want to instill in their children. They agreed on these:

Love

Being independent rather
than codependent

Honesty

Trustworthiness

Spirituality

Responsibility

Education

Mutual respect

Good manners

Open-mindedness

Kindness

Strength

Sobriety

Treating others as they want
to be treated

Gratitude

Appreciation of nature
and music

Regardless of how you were raised, I acknowledge that you have chosen positive and healthy values for you and your family. You chose recovery. Many of you are breaking a cycle and creating new and positive values. I also acknowledge you for every single healthy value that you are bringing into your family.

vaLues and Traditions

Values are the beliefs, qualities, and behaviors that you are taught, observe, and then utilize in how you relate to your world. For example, if your parents were respectful to each other and to you, you most likely grew up to be respectful. If you grew up in a home where respect was not modeled, you may have grown up not being aware that respect is important, or even know how to be respectful. If you grew up in a home where there was lots of swearing, you most likely find yourself swearing, many times without even realizing it.

You no longer have to carry any values that do not serve you. You can choose to let them go. For example, just because you were raised in a home where fighting was valued, you needn't keep that value. If respect is an important value, treat yourself respectfully. Be respectful to those around you, including your children, and it will become an important value within your family.

Traditions are information, beliefs, and customs that are handed down by word of mouth or by example from generation to generation. One mom told me that one of her earliest childhood memories was putting up her grandma's Christmas tree on Thanksgiving Day. Now that she is a mom, her family puts their tree up on that day also. She is carrying on the tradition that she experienced in her own childhood.

Teaching your children to become the loving, honest, responsible people that you want them to be begins when they are young.

It is a long process that strengthens as they grow. If your children are with you when they are young, you can begin by teaching them basic skills like brushing their teeth, helping make the bed, or feeding the dog. These small tasks are the building blocks for learning to be responsible. As children get older, age-appropriate chores are the foundation for teaching responsibility. For young children, it is not so much how well they do the chores as it is that they are learning that this is part of being a family—everyone helps. Encourage your children to do what they are capable of. Set age-appropriate expectations for them. It shows that you believe they are competent. If you need help with knowing what is age-appropriate, there are books at the bookstore or library that will give you suggestions. You'll find some in the Recommended Readings section at the end of this book.

Your children are watching you. They are learning how to do or not do many things from you. They are copying your behavior. *They learn as much or more from how you behave as from what you say.* This is why it is so important to "walk the talk."

Being a positive Role model

Do you speak to your children and others respectfully? Yelling is not being respectful. Nor is cussing or threatening. Speaking in a neutral tone is. This is one tool that will take you far in your parenting. It is not an easy skill to accomplish. You cannot expect to be respected unless you model respect for yourself and others. Do you use good manners? Say please and thank you? Do you take responsibility when you make a mistake? Do you try to learn from it? Do you take care of your possessions?

When you don't feel like going to work, do you make up an excuse to the boss that you are sick and then go out to lunch with a friend? What are you modeling? Are you teaching your children honesty or dishonesty? If you want your children to grow up to be honest and responsible, that is exactly what you need to model.

A mom of a teen recently shared with me that her daughter had called the school, saying she was ill and wouldn't be at school that day. She then called her friend, and they headed out for a day at the beach. Do you see any similarity in this scenario to calling in sick and then going out to lunch?

Frequently, I hear myself saying, *"Your habits will become their habits."* While your children learn from and respond to what you say, they also learn from and respond to how you behave. I cannot stress this enough. The following is a wonderful saying to remind you of this: *Children are watching and doing as you do, not just as you say.* I hope you will be able to see how many wonderful things you are modeling for your children—things that you may be taking for granted. As moms, we tend to see the areas where we fall short rather than the areas where we are doing well. Allow yourself to see the good in yourself. When you acknowledge your own goodness, what do you think you are modeling for your children?

Each of us influences the life of at least one child. We not only model for our own children, but for nieces, nephews, neighbors, our friends' children, and children that we don't even know, but who are watching us. Have you ever been in a store or a park and noticed how other children are watching how you interact with your children?

The following poem by Mary Rita Schilke Korzan is the first of what I call my Refrigerator Wisdom. Whenever I need a reminder or a little encouragement, I pull out this poem or others from my file and put it on the refrigerator. Glancing at it as I go through my day helps.

When You Thought I Wasn't Looking

When you thought I wasn't looking
You hung my first painting on the refrigerator
And I wanted to paint another.

When you thought I wasn't looking
You fed a stray cat
And I thought it was good to be kind to animals.

When you thought I wasn't looking
You baked a birthday cake just for me
And I knew that little things were special things.

When you thought I wasn't looking
You said a prayer
And I believed there was a God that I could always talk to.

When you thought I wasn't looking
You kissed me good-night
And I felt loved.

When you thought I wasn't looking
I saw tears come to your eyes
And I learned that sometimes things hurt—
But that it's alright to cry.

When you thought I wasn't looking
You smiled
And it made me want to look that pretty too.

When you thought I wasn't looking
You cared
And I wanted to be everything I could be.

When you thought I wasn't looking—
I looked . . .
And wanted to say, thanks
For all those things you did
When you thought I wasn't looking.

How will you touch a child's life today?

Remembering old traditions

Stephanie said, "We used to celebrate Christmas Eve at my grandma's. Christmas Day was at home. On the Fourth of July, we always had a big picnic. On Thanksgiving, we baked bread together. As soon as my kids are old enough, we are going to start these very same traditions. I also want them to get to have whatever costume they want for Halloween. It's something I always wanted when I was a kid. I didn't get it, but my kids will."

Lindsey added, "On St. Patrick's Day, my mom always made corned beef and cabbage. On Christmas, we had eggnog."

Many moms recalled how they always got to choose their favorite dinner and what kind of cake they wanted for their birthday. One teary mom offered, "I don't recall any holidays that were nice. I was either left home alone or the adults were all drunk. This is why I am trying so hard to make holidays good for my children. I want them to have happy memories of every holiday when they are my age. I think they will. We do a lot together."

Others in the group quietly nodded that they understood exactly how her holidays had been, as they had had similar experiences. Nicole shared, "For me, Easter always meant a new hat, gloves, shoes, and dress. Other holidays meant lots of people and lots of alcohol. I am doing it very differently for my son. We have people over on most holidays and share a meal and then play some games. I always try to have one that both kids and adults can play together."

Robin smiled, "I think my favorite ritual was that each of us had a special candle. Each year on our birthdays, we woke up to find the candle lit on the kitchen table. It was my mom's way of acknowledging the day. I do the same thing for my kids. Sometimes they don't say anything about it or they tell me it's corny. That's exactly what I told my mom. But the first year that I no longer was at home and there was no candle, I felt sad. It turned out to be a very special memory. It made the day important!"

creating new traditions

Keri began, "I'm new in my recovery. I haven't created any traditions or rituals with my children. I want to. We can make decorations for every holiday and put them up all over the house. I want to take them camping every summer. I want to make sure that I get their pictures taken with the Easter Bunny and with Santa. My mom always took my picture on the first day of school. I want to do that for my children too. I always grumbled and made faces at her, but I am glad today that she did it anyway."

Amber said, "I love the Fourth of July. I want to take them to watch the fireworks. On Halloween, we will dress in costumes and go trick-or-treating. I never got to do either of these things as a child, but I am going to make sure that my children do."

Jen offered, "The only tradition I remember is going to church. Christmas Eve, Christmas Day, Thanksgiving Eve, Thanksgiving Day, Easter. I was bored with all the talking, but I loved the music and the candle-lighting. I want to find a church for my family."

One of the quiet moms said, "I haven't had the chance yet, because I have been in my drug addiction. Now that I am in recovery,

I plan to be there and make these holidays happen in a way that will be a wonderful memory for my children and me. I have lots of plans for a happier future for my family."

Christina, age fifteen, said, "I love how my mom decorates the whole house. We have twinkling lights everywhere. Even though I don't help her much, I appreciate that she does it every year. On my birthday, she always makes a big deal of it. My favorite food. Presents. Sometimes even streamers and a sign.

Mark, age nine, said, "I like Easter and Fourth of July because we go to my cousins' house. They live in the country. We have an egg hunt on Easter. Sometimes, we hide the same eggs over and over just because it's fun. That's become a tradition too. On the Fourth of July, just before dark, we ride up the hill in the jeep. We can see the fireworks from all around. When they're over, we go back to my cousins' and make S'mores. It's a great tradition. Even my cousins who are in their twenties still show up."

Gail, age eleven, piped up, "Now that my mom is in recovery, we celebrate every holiday in some way. We have a big family and some of them come over. On New Year's Eve, my mom gets lots of snacks and we get to choose a movie and stay up as late as we want. Whoever is awake at midnight goes outside and hollers Happy New Year."

Tracy, age seven, said, "Every year at Christmas, my mom either makes or buys each of us a special ornament. She writes our names and the year on it. This past year, she gave me one with a soccer ball, because it's my first year of soccer. I love it. Someday, I will have a whole collection of ornaments. So far, I have seven and every year I hang all of them on the tree. My mom and I talk about each one of them. It's very fun."

Everyday Traditions and Rituals

Here is an example of an everyday tradition. It's a great way to help keep the family connected. Beth, mom of Doug, said, "Doug and I sit at the dinner table every night. Television is off. We tell each other the best thing and the hardest thing that happened that day. Even though he's almost twelve, we still read to each other at least fifteen minutes each night. I think these will both be good memories of his childhood."

Beth and Doug have created a dinner ritual that is relaxed and enjoyable. She is modeling being respectful when someone is sharing. He is getting to experience that he has a mom who is interested and listens to him.

Sometimes less is more. Less talking from mom is more beneficial and enjoyable for the relationship. *Learning to listen, really listen, to your children is a lasting gift.* It is also one that is difficult for most moms. I encourage you to try to listen without judgment or opinion. Over time, you will see that your children will share more with you. Many kids, like many moms, sometimes just want someone to hear them. They don't want or need you to fix anything or tell them what to do or not do. They simply want to be heard. This is another important skill that will take you a long way in your relationships.

I recently asked my own children what everyday traditions they remember. They told me:

Mom sitting and reading them a pile of books while they took their nightly baths.

Dad singing ridiculous songs in the car.

Always having a big orange cat named Snug. (We went through four Snugs.)

Family bike rides.

Dinner with friends every Sunday night.

My lasagna and chocolate-chip cookies.

Playing Monopoly and Uno.

You can see that my children's memories are of simple times when we were together as a family. We weren't buying them some gadget or spending a lot of money on entertainment. Distractions, like the TV, the phone, and the computer were all turned off during our family time.

If you have older or grown children, ask them what they remember about your family's everyday traditions. If you have younger children, be thinking what day-to-day traditions you are creating or want to create.

I hope this chapter has given you some good ideas for creating your own traditions and rituals.

JOURNALING ACTIVITY

1. Make a list of your top five values. Write what you are doing to instill each value in your children's lives.

2. Write about three favorite holiday traditions. What holidays are they? How do you celebrate them? With whom? How are your children involved? Ask them what traditions they like most of these three holidays?

3. Imagine that your children are grown and come home for a visit on any holiday you choose. Write what traditions, from their childhood, you want to make sure that you all get to experience during the visit.

4. What day-to-day traditions or rituals do you have with your children? Which one means the most to you and why? Which one do you think means the most to your child?

5. Write three self-acknowledgments and carry them with you through your day. Write them several times if you can. Say them out loud often.

GEMS FOR YOUR POCKET

Children learn their values from their parents.

Children learn from your behavior as much or more than they do from what you say.

Walk the talk.

Your habits will become your children's habits. Keep the ones you are proud of. What are they? Let go of the others.

Practice listening to your children.

Start creating new values and traditions—today.

You are doing many things right as a mom. Pay attention to those things and acknowledge yourself for your hard work.

Traditions do not have to cost money.

Find simple ways to remind your children that they are special and that you love them.

AFFIRMATIONS

I am proud of the values that I model for my children.

I am creating wonderful traditions for my family.

I see the goodness in me.

I see the goodness in my children.

I respect myself and others.

I am a good listener.

I am honest and trustworthy.

I am accountable for my actions.

I am strong in my recovery.

I am enough.

CHAPTER 3

Good-Bye Guilt and Shame; Hello Pride and Peace

> People are always blaming their circumstances for what
> they are. I don't believe in circumstances. The people who
> get on in this world are the people who get up and look for
> the circumstances they want and if they can't find them,
> make them.
>
> —*George Bernard Shaw*

I've never met a mom who doesn't want to be free of guilt and
shame. You may be holding beliefs about yourself from long ago.
Feelings of guilt and shame can be consuming. Imagine if you
loved and accepted yourself for exactly who you are on this very
day. Isn't that really what every mom wants?

April offered, "Sometimes I let go of my guilt and shame. First
thing you know, I've taken it all back. I wear it like a big ol' coat."
When you see that you are wearing that old coat, don't beat yourself up. Simply let it go again. Speak it, write it, pray. Do whatever
helps you to release.

Every mom wants to succeed. When you are kind and understanding with yourself, you are succeeding. As you release the
past, you feel better about yourself. You begin to experience more
joy in your life. You deserve a good life.

Every child wants to be raised without shame and guilt. It's likely that you were raised to believe mistakes were bad. When you made one, you were bad. *Mistakes are not bad. They are opportunities to learn important lessons.*

Children want to know that their parents, teachers, and other significant people in their lives are there as loving guides. Loving guides don't embarrass, humiliate, or shame children. They teach by modeling the behaviors they want to see. *Encouragement rather than discouragement benefits every child.* Your children are depending on you to teach them many of life's lessons.

Every child wants to succeed. Imagine how your self-esteem might be today if you had been parented with encouragement and acceptance rather than shame and guilt. As you continue in your recovery, you can give these gifts to your children. Every child deserves to have a safe and happy life.

Looking Back So You Can Move Forward

Some of the choices you made in the past may have inflicted punishment on you. You feel guilt and shame. You know how these feelings and beliefs came about. Hanging on to the guilt and shame benefits no one. The past is the past. You are working hard to create the life you want and deserve. You are a strong and determined woman. Let go of the past. What you do with today will lead you toward your future.

As historian Gordon Wright famously said, "The past is never completely lost, however extensive the devastation. Your sorrows are the bricks and mortar of a magnificent temple. What you are today and what you will become tomorrow are because of what you have been." Feelings of guilt and shame were likely instilled deep within you as a young child. They may still reside there. In your recovery, you are identifying them and their origin. As you release, healing continues to occur.

Many moms remember experiencing guilt and shame for the first time between the ages of three and seven. I have yet to come up with any reason that any child should ever be shamed or filled with guilt. There is just no legitimate reason for it.

Even though it is painful, many moms find it helpful to share their early memories in a safe and nonjudgmental environment. It becomes another step in their healing.

Adrianna said, "I felt so guilty when I went to my grandparents. My younger brother remained at home with my aunt. I knew she would be mean to him. I stuffed the feelings for a long time. Apologizing to him didn't help either of us. I am still ashamed that I didn't protect him."

Rachael added, "When I was seven, my mom began yelling at me and slapping me in the grocery store. People kept staring at us. I was humiliated. I didn't know what I had done wrong. I remember thinking that it must have been really bad for my mom to get so mad at me in front of everyone."

Rachael's honesty can help you see how children take on the belief that they caused their moms to be abusive. They believe that it is somehow their fault. Rachael may have done something that frustrated her mom, but that is never reason to treat any child as she described. Most likely, her mom was stressed about other things that had nothing to do with Rachael. When Rachael said the least little thing to her mom, she just blew up, unfairly spewing all of her stress onto Rachael.

Leah describes how doing what she had been taught became a source of guilt. "When I was ten," she tells us, "I got lost in the mall. I had always been told to find a policeman if I needed help. That's what I did. When my dad came to get me, he beat me badly right there in the parking lot. I felt ashamed. I was confused. I had done exactly what he had told me to do and yet I still got a beating. Later, when my mom saw my bruises, she called the police. I felt guilty for getting my dad in trouble. I was more afraid of him after that."

As a mom, you can see that Leah acted appropriately and re-sponsibly. It was her father who behaved inappropriately. What could Leah have done to protect herself? As a child, her choices were limited.

Let your children know that, if something like this happens to them—or anything that does not feel right, for that matter—they need to tell an adult who is safe and will help them. If they can't tell a parent or family member, they can tell their teachers or counselors. They need to keep telling what happened until some-one listens and believes them.

All too often, a child's true experience is denied by adults. Sometimes the adults simply don't want to deal with it. They choose to remain in denial. Children need to hear from you over and over that looking for help is the right thing to do, even though it may be hard at the time. If your children share something with you, even if you don't fully believe them or you don't want to think that the person they are talking about would harm them in any way, you need to find out what actually did or didn't happen. *It is your responsibility as their mom not to deny, but instead to inves-tigate. You are your children's advocate and protector.*

My friend Rebecca often says, "Doing the right thing does not always feel right in the moment." It is not your children's respon-sibility to protect anyone who is harming them or anyone else. If there is someone in your life that is abusive to you or your chil-dren in any way, protect all of you by not allowing that person to be in your lives. Find the resources and support that you need.

Do not fall into the trap of feeling that you have to defend or protect anyone who is harming or abusing any of you. Once again, *your fidelity needs to be to your children. Keeping your children safe, is a vital part of being a mom.*

understanding and supporting yourself

Many women—moms, and definitely moms in recovery—tend to be hard on themselves. This is never helpful to you or anyone else. Learning to be kind and understanding to yourself is often challenging.

How do you treat your best friend or your favorite person in the whole world? Do you put them down? Tell them they are losers? Shame them when they make a mistake? I doubt it. I am strongly encouraging you to begin treating yourself with gentleness and understanding, just as you do your best friend.

"I would never say anything to hurt my best friend's feelings," one mom said. "We help each other as much as we can. Recently, we were walking down the street and a complete stranger made a sarcastic remark about her outfit. Her feelings were hurt. No matter what I said, she hung on to the hurtful words of the stranger. She continued to berate herself as though he were right. She is much more apt to take in negative than positive comments. One negative comment can ruin a whole day."

Josie added, "My aunt is my favorite person. She raised me. Sometimes, she makes mistakes with her own children. She then spends the next week beating herself up and telling everyone what a bad mom she is. I encourage her instead to sit down and listen to her kids, even if she doesn't agree with them. The other day, her oldest daughter was upset. My aunt took her for a drive, just the two of them. By the time they got back, they both felt better. My aunt did not beat herself up. She did learn that, especially with teens, sometimes it's helpful to go for a drive. They don't have to sit and look at you directly, and many times, this helps them open up and share their thoughts and feelings." *We all need to have someone in our lives who listens to us.*

Here are some simple ways to be gentle with yourself:

1. **Stop:** Catch yourself as soon as you begin to beat yourself up.

2. **Breathe:** Pause and take a few deep breaths.

3. **Pray:** Ask your higher power to help you.

4. **Have compassion:** Picture yourself holding a newborn baby or an animal you love.

5. **Speak from your heart:** Reassure yourself that you are okay.

6. **Use affirmations:** Replace negative thoughts with positive ones.

7. **Let it go:** Nudge yourself to release and forgive.

8. **Let it go again:** If it returns, just let it go again.

By the time you do some or all of these, you will be treating yourself in a more gentle way. It will feel foreign at first. Keep practicing. Think, pray, speak with gentleness. You will come to know this part of you. What a wonderful skill to be modeling for your children. They can grow up treating themselves with the kindness and compassion that everyone deserves. Sometimes, we forget who we truly are. Some of you may not yet have discovered that person within yourself. Take a moment and imagine how your higher power may see you. Review the affirmations at the end of this chapter. Choose one and let it become your mantra. Speak the words over and over, until you shift into a peaceful, loving place. Writing the affirmation can help. See what happens. You may be pleasantly surprised.

Bribery

There are many reasons why moms sometimes resort to bribery and trying to buy love and respect. Often, it is out of guilt—guilt for your behaviors when you were in your addiction. Many of you have told me that you think that, if you buy your children things, they will love you more. They will forgive you for the past hurts and disappointments. At other times, you may feel that they are out of control and you don't know what to do. If you bribe them to do what you want, maybe they will quit acting out.

Sometimes you resort to bribery out of desperation. You've tried every tactic you know. Nothing is working. You are frustrated, embarrassed, and exhausted. Here are some examples of predicaments that you may have found yourself in.

APRIL AND HER M&MS

It's time for the daily struggle of getting April into her car seat. Her mom, Janice, offers her a little bag of M&Ms if she will just get into her seat and buckle up. It works! What child would turn down a bag of M&Ms? Janice and April are happily on their way. The next morning, April once again refuses to get into her seat. Janice is frustrated. She's going to be late for work. April doesn't care. "Where's my M&Ms?" she asks. Janice says she doesn't have any today. April is really mad. Equally angry, Janice struggles with April until she finally gets her buckled in. They drive to school. April cries and whines all the way. She gets out of the car and slams the door, refusing to say good-bye. Both April and Janice begin their day upset and frustrated.

Bribing sometimes works in the moment, as it did that fateful day when Janice first offered the bag of M&Ms. April learned quickly that her mom would give her a treat if she was "good." She learned that, if Janice wanted her cooperation, she could force her to give her something. April was missing out on learning an important life skill—cooperation, doing the right thing because it's the right thing to do, not because she will get something.

The main reason for the car seat is April's safety. Mom had not thought of explaining this to April at some time other than when they were in their daily power struggle. April was old enough that she would have understood her mother's reasoning. She probably would have been more cooperative once she understood why she had to be buckled up. Many power struggles can be eliminated simply by taking the time to explain to your children why something is important.

A TOY A WEEK

Sometimes a mom resorts to bribery because she thinks it will help relieve her guilt. You may feel bad that you did not parent your children effectively while you were in your addiction. If you buy them things now, they will love you more. You will feel less guilty. Many can attest to the fact that this is incorrect. *Your children are not going to forgive you any sooner or love you more because you buy them things.*

Terry shared this story: "I got into the habit of having a present for my kids every time they came for a visit. They soon grew to expect it. They didn't even say hi or hug me when they first arrived. 'Where's my present?' was their greeting. I felt both angry and hurt. I realized that I was setting us all up. I decided to change my behavior. The next visit began with yelling and pouting. I was frustrated. They were mad because there was no present. In my parenting class, I realized that I was buying them things because I still have so much guilt. I somehow thought I could buy their love. I could make up for lost time. I learned that buying them something did not lessen my guilt. In fact, I think it added to my guilt.

It wasn't making them love me any more. I want them to learn that us getting to be together is the gift."

Terry has a new plan for the next visit. She is going to have something organized and ready that will be fun for all of them. Maybe it will be a board game all set up. Maybe some buckets and shovels ready for digging—any kind of activity that will help get them get engaged with one another.

While your children may initially grumble that there isn't a present that day, they will find this gift meaningful and lasting. An hour, a day, or a week from now, they most likely will not remember any of the toys you bought them. They will remember how you spent time with them during those visits. You will most likely also feel better about yourself and the time you have with your child.

I WANT IT AND I WANT IT NOW!

Many moms tell me that, when they take their children to the store, all they hear is "I want. I want." Martha told us how she used to let her children pick out something every time they went to a store, even if she couldn't afford it. "I didn't know how to say that I didn't have enough money," she explained. "Sometimes, I put off paying my utility bill to buy them what they wanted. I, like Terry, thought it might make up for the time that I wasn't there for them. I was also afraid of how mad they would be if I didn't get them something. When I did try to say 'No, not today,' they began yelling and crying. I used to get mad and yell back. They said things that hurt my feelings. Eventually, I broke down and bought them something. They have learned that, if they yell and scream long enough, they will win. I feel helpless at these times. I was teaching them that, if they want something, they need to just keep misbehaving until I give in. They are learning the art of manipulation. In truth, I am the one teaching it to them."

Martha's solution? "Now, before we go into a store," she says, "I tell them exactly what we are buying. I try to include them in the shopping. I may ask them to find a certain item, put five apples in the bag, or check off the items on the list as we put them in the cart. I find that, when I involve them more in the shopping, they are much more cooperative. If they do throw a fit, I leave the cart. Trying to stay calm, I bring them outside or to the car. I am not being rough or saying anything. I get them to a place where they can calm themselves down."

Remember, when your children are screaming or crying, they can't hear anything. This is not the time to try to reason with them. "I am teaching them by my action," Martha says, "rather than with words. After making them leave the store three times, my two sons got the message. They helped me find what we went in to get and asked if maybe next time they could have something. I am proud of all three of us."

Martha learned two important lessons here:

1. **Plan ahead.** Tell the kids before going into the store what you are there to buy. For example, "Today, we are buying your cousin's birthday gift, milk, and bread. That is all."

2. **Set expectations.** Tell them in a firm and kind voice exactly what you expect of them. "I expect you to walk next to me, holding on to the cart. I also expect you to talk in your indoor voice while we are in the store."

Your children want to please you. They want your approval. Your trip to the store is apt to be more enjoyable for everyone if you have let them know what the plan is and what you expect of them ahead of time.

TEENAGE EXTORTION

Using a few candies, a little toy, or your spare change may appear harmless when your child is young. But before you know it, your children are teenagers and your childhood currency is no longer enough. They not only want more; they expect more. Instead of a little toy, they want an expensive toy. They will no longer settle for a dollar. As they get older, they will laugh in your face if you offer them anything less than a twenty.

Nina talks about the results she got from bribing: "At first, bribing them worked great. In the long run, it isn't great at all. Now that they are old enough to help with chores, they refuse to do anything unless I pay them. I don't have the money. I can't make them do anything. I feel sad when I say this. I didn't realize that I was teaching them this behavior. They are so lazy. Their only incentive these days is money. I completely missed out on teaching them that this is part of being a family."

Cheril is the mom of three daughters, ages ten, thirteen, and fifteen. "When I was in my addiction," she tells us, "I would pay them to go away for a few hours. I didn't care where. I just wanted them out of the house. Today, they use this as a bargaining chip. I get so frustrated and yet I know where it came from. This pattern is really hard to turn around at their ages."

Abbey spoke up. "In the past, all it did was break me. This prolonged my struggle and added to my problems as well as theirs. I would buy them what they wanted with the rent money. As soon as we got home, the thing that they had to have just minutes ago was thrown in the corner with the rest of the toys. I ended up mad at them for not taking care of the new item. They knew that, the next time we went to the store, they would get something else. There was no need to take care of anything. They grew up unappreciative—not just of me, but of gifts from their grandparents too. Without realizing it, I taught them that they could have whatever they wanted whenever they wanted it, regardless of whether or not I could afford it. They did not learn to respect and care for their things."

It is important for you to understand what your children are learning when you use bribery. They are learning that, if someone wants them to do something, all that person needs to do is to pay them in some way. They are missing out on learning the importance of cooperation and responsibility. They are missing out on the opportunity to do the right thing because it's right, not because they get something out of it. They are being cheated out of the good feeling and the higher self-esteem that comes from cooperative and responsible behavior.

Guilt and shame

Children who are raised with guilt and shame tend to lack confidence in themselves. They believe what they have been told by their parents.

Jacob, now a teenager, said, "When I was young, I was repeatedly told that my parents drank because of me." He believed it. He felt that he was the problem. It affected his self-esteem and his relationships, not only with his parents, but with his peers. It was hard for him to make friends. He felt as if he didn't fit in anywhere.

Fortunately, in Jacob's junior year, he had a teacher who saw his potential. Throughout the year, they talked. Jacob came to realize that he was not the reason for his parents' alcoholism. His teacher helped him see the good in himself. By the end of the year, Jacob had created a small group of friends and felt much better about himself. His home life was no different, except that he no longer let anyone put guilt or shame on him.

Jacob admitted that, at first, it was hard for him to trust his teacher. He had never had anyone who believed in him. "At first, when my teacher started talking to me about being all that I could be, I felt confused. I had been a victim for as long as I could remember. Now this teacher is telling me that I am much more than that. If I am not a victim, what am I? I had always been told that I was not good enough or smart enough. I would never amount to anything. I believed it all. I had not learned to trust anyone. How can I trust what this person is telling me?"

Many children parented with guilt and shame experience anxiety and depression. It can begin at an early age and continue until they get professional guidance and support. If you are concerned that your child may be experiencing anxiety or depression, consult a doctor or therapist. We do not want any child to suffer needlessly.

Many moms have told me how resentful and angry they became once they realized the amount and depth of shame and guilt they carried. In a parenting class, we talked about the incentives for keeping guilt and shame. The list was pretty short. Everyone in the group agreed that there aren't really many benefits—if any. Here's what a few of them had to say:

"It's a reminder of where I came from."

"You don't have to face your past, what you did."

"You don't have to change your behaviors."

"My guilt and shame bring me down and keep me in my depression."

Everyone agreed that letting go of all guilt and shame is the way to go.

So then, we began to list behaviors that can help people let go of guilt and shame. See which ones are helpful to you. Maybe there are some that you have never thought to try.

I pray for help.

I change my behaviors.

When I release guilt and shame, I feel better. My confidence and hope build.

I write in my journal.

I refuse to listen to negativity. I walk away.

I cry a lot.

I realize what I am doing and stop doing it.

I face the truth.

I face the consequences, no matter how hard it is, or how much it hurts, or how scared I may be. I feel so much better once I do. I gain peace of mind and a sense of accomplishment.

I talk about it with my sponsor, a friend, or my counselor.

Now that I'm in recovery, I tell myself positive things about myself every day.

I put guilt and shame behind me by making better decisions. The good decisions replace the guilt.

I change my thoughts.

The amount of wisdom in this list is astounding. I encourage you to turn back to this page the next time you need a little help letting go of some old guilt and shame. Better yet, write out the list on a piece of paper and make your own Refrigerator Wisdom from it.

JOURNALING ACTIVITY

1. At what age do you first remember experiencing shame and guilt? Write the memory briefly. What did you do with that memory? What were the feelings? Was there anyone there to protect you?

2. Now write how you would have liked that experience to occur.

3. What do you know about your guilt and shame as a mom? How does it show up? What do you do with it? What tools do you use to disperse it?

4. What has been your experience with bribery and buying your way out of guilt? How do you feel during these times? How do your feel afterward? How do you think your child feels?

5. What tools do you use to help you refrain from bribery?

6. What do you do to "let go" of guilt and shame? How do you feel when you have released it? When it creeps back in, what do you do?

7. As you release these old feelings of guilt and shame and the beliefs that came along with them, what feelings and beliefs replace them?

Be kind and gentle to yourself. Regardless of past beliefs about yourself, you are deserving.

Mistakes are not bad. They are opportunities to learn important life lessons.

Let go of your guilt and shame.

Whenever it reappears, let it go again.

Make good choices. What you do with today will lead you toward your future.

Teach your children that, if someone is hurting them, they need to tell a safe adult. If that person does not believe them, they need to keep telling until someone believes and helps them.

Bribery may appear to work in the moment. It does not work in the long run.

When you find yourself resorting to bribery, think of a more effective way to parent.

Plan ahead. When going somewhere with your children, tell them ahead of time exactly what is going to happen and what you expect of them. Make sure that your expectations are realistic.

Follow through on your word.

AFFIRMATIONS

I am free of guilt and shame.

I am kind and gentle with myself and those around me.

I release any and all past beliefs that are not true to who I am.

The past is the past. I forgive myself as well as others.

I learn from my mistakes.

I deserve to have a joyful and healthy life.

I am creating my life as I want it to be.

I love and accept myself for exactly who I am.

I am strong in my recovery.

I am enough.

CHAPTER 4

Handling Anger—Yours and Your Child's

> If children live with hostility,
> they learn to fight.
> If children live with encouragement,
> they learn confidence.

—Dorothy Law Nolte

Every mom wants to succeed. Remaining in recovery and creating a full and satisfying life are important. Being the best mom you can be is no easy undertaking. Modeling positive ways of being in your world help you build solid and loving relationships with your children. For many children, you are the most significant role model in their lives.

What are some of the behaviors that you model for your children that make you proud? Maybe it's having a job, or paying your rent and bills on time, or helping a friend who is ill or needs a ride. Maybe it's expressing your feelings, even when you are angry, in a healthy way that does not hurt anyone. By these behaviors, you model responsibility, accountability, time management, how to be a friend, and lending a hand to someone in need.

All moms want to remain calm even when their children are screaming, crying, or acting out. Sometimes, it can feel almost impossible to know what to do. Finding ways other than those with which you were most likely parented is important. Having tools that will help you release your feelings of frustration and anger in an effective way will make you feel better about yourself as a mom. At the same time, it will teach your children how to handle their anger in healthy ways that will not hurt or harm anyone else.

Children want to feel safe and loved. They want moms who will take care of them, provide food, shelter, and clothing, and understand them. They want moms who teach them right from wrong, moms who respect themselves as well as their kids. Having a mom who handles her frustration, stress, and anger in healthy ways is important. *Children learn how to handle their anger by watching those around them.*

Have you ever noticed that, if you are a yeller, your children are most likely yellers too. If you tend to swat or spank them, they will do the same aggressive acts, not only to you, but to others when they are mad. If you take a "cooling off" time when you're angry, you model that behavior for them and teach them to do the same.

As psychotherapist Richard J. Delaney, Ph.D. says, "When kids are acting their worst, that's when they need you the most." Like everyone, children want to be accepted, not rejected.

Looking Back So You Can Move Forward

Many of you were not raised by parents who knew positive ways to handle their feelings. As I said in chapter 1, we do what we know and when we know better, we do better. Your parents used the tools they had at the time.

This book is about you, a mom, today. You can learn new and more effective ways to handle anger. I recently asked a group of moms how their parents handled anger. Here are their responses:

Yelling at each other and us kids, actually anyone who was in their way

Hitting, spanking, beating, threatening, put-downs

Drugs and alcohol

Intimidation

They stormed out of the house, leaving us alone for hours.

They ignored me and just turned on the TV.

Sarcasm

They locked me in my room with no dinner.

Name-calling

They withheld any conversation for days.

When we finished the list, I asked the question, "Is there any positive method on this list?" I received an immediate and unanimous "No." Since this is how their parents modeled handling anger, this, of course, is what they learned to do when they were angry.

Fortunately today, there are positive and reinforcing ways for parents to learn to cope with such feelings more effectively. There are many tools and techniques that you can use when you are angry that will not harm or diminish your children's self-esteem.

what is Anger?

Anger is a natural and healthy feeling. Everyone gets angry. Things happen that cause you to react emotionally. Anger is one of your emotions. Please remember that your children are learning how to handle their feelings from you. Scary, isn't it? It's how you handle your anger that can be either positive or negative.

Anger is a signal to you and those around you that something is wrong. It can help you make a change in some area of your life so you can move forward. It can help keep you safe in a dangerous situation. We all need help sometimes handling these intense feelings of anger.

How long you choose to hang on to the anger is up to you. The sooner you let go of angry feelings, the better for everyone involved—mostly yourself. *Your anger hurts you more than it affects anyone else.*

Here's how I addressed anger in one group. I told them all to imagine a quilt spread out in front of them. The quilt represents anger. "When you look under the quilt," I asked, "what do you find?" An almost immediate shift took place in the room. The room echoed with the words, "disappointment, hurt, fear."

We began another list that we called, "How I handle my anger":

Yelling, sarcasm, put-downs

Hitting, tantrums, punching

Leaving

Stuffing and then exploding

Passive-aggressive behavior

Picking a physical fight

Spankings

Throwing and breaking things

Johanna spoke up and said, "Why don't we just list everything on our parents list and that is our list too." No one was surprised at the similarities.

chiLdren and Your Anger

When you lose your temper with your children, one of two things happens for them. They think, "Uh-oh, mom's out of control. What's going to happen to me?" The feeling is almost always one of fear. Or "Uh-oh, mom's out of control. I'm in charge." Children, especially older ones, sometimes act and talk as though they want to be in charge. In truth, they don't, nor is it good for them. They need and deserve to be kids. They deserve to have happy and safe childhoods.

Margo, mom of three, said, "I am so embarrassed, but when I start yelling, they curl up, hold their ears, and look so afraid of me. At the time, I don't care. It doesn't stop me from yelling. Later, saying I'm sorry does not take away the hurt. I only recently learned that, every time I yell at them, their self-esteem goes down. I feel awful."

Rochelle, mom of a toddler, hesitantly shared, "When I get mad, her little face looks so confused and afraid." Tears came to Rochelle's eyes. "I love her more than anyone else on this earth. How can she be afraid of me?"

Diana added, "My kids are teenagers now. When I start yelling or threatening, they get right in my face and yell back and then eventually storm off. They usually leave the house and don't return for hours. I worry. I think sometimes they stay away not so much to cool off, but to punish me. It feels like revenge, because I began the screaming match. When they do return, we either get into another fight or we don't talk about the earlier disagreement. Nothing ever changes with us. It's really hard when they get to be this age. I can't just carry them off to their rooms anymore. Their anger actually scares me. I'm seeing how they have felt all those years when

I lost my temper. Sometimes, my oldest son will just laugh in my face as he storms out the door. I feel so low at these times."

A mom with newborn twins said, "I am so tired. I just realized that, when I get frustrated about anything, they usually get fussy. Their pediatrician said they are probably picking up on my tension. Who ever said that being a mom was going to be easy? Why don't they come up with some kind of a manual?"

I imagine most every mom has asked herself that very question at some point in her parenting. And while they haven't come up with a manual, the good news is that there are more resources, educational materials, and support today than your parents most likely had. You'll find some of it in the Recommended Readings section at the end of this book.

chiLdren and Their Anger

Then we made a third list based on the question "How do your children handle their anger?":

Yelling, hitting, put-downs

Tantrums

The silent treatment

Running away

Crying

Throwing things, breaking things

Slamming doors

Pouting

Saying hurtful things

Isolating themselves

There it was in black and white. Three generations handling anger in very similar ways. Take a moment and reflect on how your own children handle their anger? Is there a similarity between your way and theirs?

Ten-year-old Liz said, "When I get mad, I go cry somewhere peaceful. Sometimes I start reading. I bite my nails."

Eric, age seven, quietly offered, "Yesterday, I got mad at my mom. I kicked my baby brother when I walked by him because I wanted to get even with mom. The baby cried, and I got in even more trouble. Plus, I felt bad for doing that to my brother."

Angie, age sixteen, shared this: "When mom starts in, I just say something mean and leave. I go to a friend's house or find something to do until I am not mad anymore."

Bill, age thirteen, told me, "My mom took my bedroom door off because I kept slamming it every time she made me mad. Now I'm really mad. I have no privacy. I haven't spoken to her in four days. She slams doors a lot, and it's not fair that she can do it but I can't."

Before we go any further, take a sheet of paper or grab your journal. Make three columns: "My parents," "Me," "My child." Make a list of how each one handles their frustration and anger. When you finish, see how many are the same or similar. Highlight or circle any behaviors that you want to keep.

MY PARENTS	ME	MY CHILD

Learning to handle anger in a more positive way will benefit both you and your child. *You can change the course of how your family has most likely handled anger for generations. You can break the cycle.*

Life coach and *O* magazine contributor Martha Beck has said, "Allowing children to show their guilt, show their grief, show their anger takes the sting out of a situation." It's your job as a parent to provide your children with safe and healthy ways to handle their feelings.

cooling off

We've talked about what anger is, about patterns passing from generation to generation. Now we are ready to move forward to learn some new, effective ways to handle anger and the effects these methods will likely have on you and your children.

Be very gentle with yourself. These changes do not occur overnight. Every time you handle an angry moment in a new way, you are integrating that way of being into your life. Modeling new, more effective ways to handle anger shows your children how they can begin to handle their own anger. You will soon see that you feel better about yourself. Your children will begin responding to you differently. They may begin to show their anger in more positive ways.

In one workshop, we decided to have some fun adding new tools to our parenting toolbox. Moms need to have fun too. I put some positive phrases that described healthy ways to handle anger on little sheets of paper. One by one, the moms took them and had the choice of either acting out the phrase or drawing it on the board. Here are some of the scenarios and their responses.

EXIT OR WAIT

The first phrase required two moms—one to play the mom and one to play the child. In the scenario, the child has just spilled her second glass of milk at the dinner table. Mom is ready to explode. Instead of yelling and ranting and raving, she says nothing and leaves the kitchen. She is using a strategy we call *exit or wait*. When you can, simply remove yourself until you have calmed down. Many times, it's the mom who needs the "cooling down" time rather than the child. Wash your face, count to ten, or to 100 if necessary, walk outside—anything that will help you let go of the anger. There is no point in saying anything until you have calmed down.

If you have children that are too young to be left alone for any amount of time and no other adult is present, you sometimes have to get creative. Maybe the best you can do is to say nothing and take some deep breaths. Try drinking a glass of water. Maybe it's the perfect time to quietly say the Serenity Prayer. "God, grant me the serenity...."

Many times, it isn't really about the spilled milk at all. It's the final straw in a day of stress, frustration, and exhaustion. By removing yourself until you are calm, you avoid taking out the angry feelings that have been building up all day long on your child. Try to be aware of what is really causing your stress or anger. When you have this awareness, it will help you avoid the trap of taking those feelings out on your child.

BREATHE

The next mom stood up and didn't say anything. She just quietly stood there, taking deep breaths. Before long, someone said, "Breathe." Everyone laughed and said, "Oh yeah. We always forget about that one." The good news is that breathing costs no money. It's always with you. You can access it as often as you like. In fact, if you paused four times a day and took the time to do ten deep-breathing cycles, you would feel less stressed.

By the time my daughter was three, she sometimes looked at my face and said, "Mommy, I think you need to take some deep breaths." She was absolutely right. She was feeling and seeing my frustrations building up, sometimes even before I was aware of them. When my kids were about two-and-a-half, I began what they thought was a wonderful game. "Let's join hands and take some deep breaths." They loved it, because it was playful to them. I was connecting with them, and they were also shifting their own energy to a happier more relaxed place.

For young children, as you breathe in, it's fun to say, "Smell the roses"; as you breathe out, say "blow out the candles." There's a card in my office that says simply, "Breathe." It's a great reminder for all of us.

Recently, I was making a home visit to a family who had four children between the ages of six and seventeen. Everyone in the family was trying to learn more positive ways to handle their anger. On a prior visit, we had talked about breathing. I walked in, and they were all chuckling. They had made thirty-seven little signs that all read "Breathe!" and put them up all over the house. On the mirrors, on doors, in the hallway, on the refrigerator. You name it, it had a sign on it that said, "Breathe!" This had been a fun family project, seeing who could make the most creative sign. It was also a great reminder of the tool that costs nothing and is always with them. They could not believe how much less yelling and arguing there had been since the signs went up. They left the signs up for nearly a year.

You are working hard as you read this chapter. Take a moment, put your book down, and just take ten deep breaths. Notice how you feel before and after. Are you a little more relaxed?

Quick activity: Take a piece of paper. Make your own "Breathe!" sign. When my kids were still at home, I often had little Post-it notes saying "Breathe" above every phone, every mirror, even in my car. It helped to have a visual reminder. You may also want to turn this into a family-night project and make some signs like the family above did.

EXERCISE

Next, we have the mom who drags in exhausted from work. The house is a mess; chores are not done; dinner's not started; TV and music are roaring. Sound familiar? She changes her clothes and gets on her treadmill. "Exercise," they all say. Many moms share that, when they exercise regularly, they feel less stressed and don't lose their tempers as much. This mom was wise. Her old way might have been to come in the door and start hollering at everyone.

ASK FOR HELP WHEN YOU NEED IT

Next, one of the moms with a newborn in her arms and another mom come up front. The mom with the baby is clearly frustrated, teary, and exhausted. She asks the other mom if she can take the baby for a couple of hours. The other mom happily does. The frustrated new mom goes back to her room, takes a shower, and has a nap.

For many women, it is hard to ask for support, whether it be to get a break from the baby, a ride somewhere, or a meal cooked. If this mom had not asked her friend to take the baby, she might have ended up taking her frustrations out on the child, which is something no mother ever wants to do.

As any mom knows, it is amazing how just a couple of hours can replenish you enough to get you through another day. Once you've had a break, you will most likely be happy to reconnect with your child.

For many of us, it is far easier to lend a hand and help our friends than it is to be the one who asks for the help. Over the years, I have learned that, in truth, giving and receiving are the same thing. When you give something to another, you receive something at the same time. When you ask your friend for help, you receive support, but you also give that friend the gift of the good feelings that come with giving.

"I" NOT "YOU"

Think of the last time you were angry with someone. Let's say your partner is supposed to be home at 5:30 and strolls in after 7:00. You might start off saying, "I am so mad that you are late. I'm disappointed that I had to miss my class tonight because you didn't come home to be with the kids. You have ruined another dinner hour and evening for everyone. You don't ever think of anyone but yourself. You always do this, and it makes me mad every time you do."

Notice how, in the first two sentences, she used "I" statements. "I am mad. I am disappointed." Then she almost immediately shifted into "you" statements. "You" statements feel accusatory to the other person and typically make the person defensive. That's when the argument begins.

When your child makes you angry, what is your usual response? "You make me so mad. Why are you being such a brat? How could you have left your bike outside? You just don't think. What is wrong with you?"

Sound familiar? When you say things like this, your children most likely hear that they are unacceptable, not that the behavior is unacceptable. Yes, sometimes your children's behavior is unacceptable, but children are never bad. "You" statements can hurt.

Children take on the belief that they are bad because their moms get mad at them. Their self-esteem is affected every time this happens.

"I" statements tell children how you feel without blaming anyone. They don't diminish their self-esteem. When you are angry, try saying, "I'm so mad" rather than "You make me so mad." Remember, only you can choose how you feel about any situation. No one can make you mad unless that is what you choose to feel.

By age three, your children can put words to their feelings. "I am mad! I am frustrated." You can help them by acknowledging their feelings and helping them find the words to express them rather than acting out in some other ineffective way. You might say, "I see how mad you are. It is hard when you don't get to play with the big kids, isn't it?"

Tell your children what they can do with their anger. "You can use your words to tell the big kids how you feel. You can go outside and scream. Maybe you'd like to draw me an angry picture." If they are not able to decide what they want to do, you may need to help them. If your children don't like any of your suggestions and can't come up with any on their own, you may want to help them get to a safe, quiet place until they have cooled down.

After both of you have calmed down, you can talk about what happened and how they might handle it next time.

staying in the moment

Let's go back to the glass of spilled milk. How frustrated do you really need to be over a glass of spilled milk? If you were not exhausted, stressed, worried, and angry, it would probably not be a big deal at all. However, when it is the end of the day and you're tired and stressed, it is easy to lose perspective. Three ounces of spilled milk becomes the final straw.

The following is an exaggeration, but I want you to understand how it might feel to a child when you allow one spill to bring up past spills. Have you ever heard yourself saying something like this? "Once again, you have ruined our dinner time. It's the only time we get to sit down with your dad and now it's ruined. You do this every night. Why do I even give you anything to drink? It's just like last Christmas at Nana's when you spilled your milk and ruined Christmas dinner for everyone. The year before, you did the very same thing at Uncle Bill's and ruined Easter. We cannot even take you anywhere! Why are you always so clumsy?"

Get the idea? *Mom is blowing off steam from her stressful day. The child's self-esteem is sinking lower with each sentence and accusation that is spewed.* Stay in the present moment. Once again, how mad do you really need to get over a few ounces of spilled milk? Not very.

If you are in touch with what is really bothering you, you will be less apt to take it out on your child. Moms frequently ask me, "So what am I supposed to do when they spill their milk?"

First, my rule of thumb is to put in the cup only what you are willing to wipe up. In other words, don't give young children six ounces of milk all at once. Give them two. When they are done with that, give them two more. If they still spill, hand them a paper towel and, as you are wiping it up, have them help you—not as a punishment, but as a way of teaching them that, when you spill something, this is how you take care of it. With older kids, say in a neutral tone, "There's the paper towel. Please wipe it up and then get yourself some more milk." *Using a neutral tone is a vital key to parenting.*

warning, Threats, and Force

Warnings and threats are not the same. A threat usually has something punitive within it. You may or may not follow through.

For example, you may say, "If you don't get your room cleaned up right now, I am canceling your birthday party." I suppose some parents might actually cancel the party, but most wouldn't. In your desperation to get the child to do the chore, you resort to idle threats. Young children may, out of fear, get busy and clean their rooms. However, very soon, they come to know that you won't follow through. "She always threatens stuff, but she never does it."

What can you learn from this? You don't want your children to be afraid of you. You want them to learn to be responsible, trustworthy, and respectful. When you give idle threats, your children learn that they cannot trust what you say and that you are not being respectful to them. How can you teach them these values if you are not modeling them? You can't.

A warning is exactly what the word says. A statement telling children what you expect of them and what the consequence will be if they do not follow through.

For example: "The sand belongs in the bucket. If you throw the sand at anyone else, it will be time to go home." You are telling them exactly what you expect, as well as the consequence. If they make a poor choice and throw the sand, you needn't even start giving them a lecture. Simply pick up your items, hand them whatever they need to carry, and head for the car. They will learn far more by you taking this action than by your lecturing them or letting them have another chance. They will learn through natural and logical consequences. Following through in what you say shows respect, and that you will do what you say. For most kids, the more you practice giving one warning and following through, the sooner they improve their behaviors.

Quick Activity: Grab a piece of paper or your journal. Read each statement below and write down whether you think it's a threat or a warning.

1. You can either finish your dinner or go to bed now.

2. If you come in past your curfew tonight, consider yourself grounded for the rest of the semester.

3. If you come in past your curfew tonight, you'll be staying home tomorrow night.

4. You can jump in the pool three more times, and then we're leaving.

5. If you don't finish your homework this afternoon, you can't go out tonight.

6. If you lose your jacket again, you'll have to find something else to wear.

7. If you lose your jacket again, I'm not ever buying you another one.

8. If you say that word again, you'll be writing "I will not say that again" 500 times.

9. If you say that word again, you'll be going outside or to your room.

10. Tell Grandma you are sorry or go get the bar of soap. You know what I'll do with that.*

As for using force to discipline a child, I like what Nancy Samalin says in her book, *Love and Anger: The Parental Dilemma*: "If spanking worked, we'd only have to do it once. When you've won by asserting physical power as a big person over a small person, you've won nothing."

Many moms have said to me, "I got spanked and I came out alright." My response is, "You came out alright not because you were spanked, but in spite of it."

Here's how I answered the questions: threats—1, 2, 7, 8, 10; warnings—3, 4, 5, 6, 9.

I have spoken to thousands of moms on this very issue. My bottom line question is always: "Why would a mom ever want to hit these little people that we love more than anyone else in the world? It makes no sense when you think about it."

Many a parent has cried when they heard this, because it resonates within their hearts. This is why it is so important that all moms learn to handle their anger in more appropriate and positive ways.

Cynthia said, "I don't spank. I just swat them or pinch their shoulder a little too hard to let them know they are doing something wrong." Whether it's a swat on the hand, a spanking, a pinch, biting, soap in the mouth, Tabasco sauce on the tongue, it all hurts and attacks self-esteem. Many children, after being reprimanded in this way, think, "I must really be a bad girl because mommy had to hit me," or "I don't know what I did wrong, but I know I am bad because I made mom mad." *Every time children are reprimanded in any of these ways, it changes who they are.* No amount of words can take the hurt away.

JOURNALING ACTIVITY

I.   List five ways you can handle your anger that you think will be more positive and effective for you and your children.

2.   Write about a time when you lost your temper with your child. Then write how you can do it differently the next time.

3.   Write at least three self-acknowledgments. Carry them with you throughout your day or put them somewhere that you will see them often. I know how hard it is to be the mom that you want to be. Giving yourself acknowledgments

helps you continue to make the changes that you are working so hard to make. I'll get you started. "I acknowledge myself for taking some deep breaths today instead of immediately yelling at my kids."

4. Take some index cards or a piece of paper and make some reminders that you can put around the house. For example, "Breathe," "Neutral tone," "Exit or wait." This will most likely also peak your children's interest and can serve as a gentle reminder for them to do the same thing.

GEMS FOR YOUR POCKET

Breathe. Four times a day, pause long enough to take ten deep breaths.

Use a neutral tone.

When you hear yourself not using a neutral tone, quiet yourself until you are calm once again.

Exercise regularly.

It is a wise mom who knows when she needs some help and asks for it. Maybe it's a friend, a family member, your sponsor. The important thing is to ask.

Speak in the "I" voice, not the "You" voice. This way, you are taking responsibility for your own feelings, thoughts, and actions.

Stay in the moment. Don't bring up past misbehaviors. Address only what is happening now.

Find other ways to react besides physical force, threats, and bribes.

Pray. Meditate.

Choose your battles. It's too exhausting for both of you if you battle over every little thing.

Be consistent.

Write your feelings.

When you are frustrated, instead of yelling or acting out, count.

GEMS TO HELP CHILDREN HANDLE THEIR ANGER

Validate their anger and help them put a name to their feelings.

Tell them what they can do with their anger. For example:
Go outside and scream, draw a mad picture, stomp your feet.

Walk away until your child has a chance to cool down.

If it's needed, help them get to a quiet place where they can regroup themselves.

While they are cooling off, it is important that you do the same thing.

Once both of you are in a calm place, talk about how it could be done differently next time. Don't lecture them.

Do your best to model appropriate ways to handle anger.

Catch them handling their anger well and acknowledge it.
"I appreciate you using kind words when you asked to go into your brother's room, even though you are mad that he said no."

AFFIRMATIONS

I am peaceful and calm even when my life appears full of chaos.

I handle my stress and anger in healthy ways.

When I first feel my anger, I am reminded to let go.

I talk to my children respectfully.

I listen to my children daily.

I choose my battles appropriately.

I am consistent in my parenting.

I acknowledge myself and my children daily.

I am strong in my recovery.

I am enough.

CHAPTER 5

Forgiving and Letting Go

> We may not know how to forgive, and we may not want to forgive;
> but the very fact we say we are willing to forgive begins the heal-
> ing practice.
>
> *—Louise Hay*

You most likely have wounds that began when you were very young.
Every mom wants to heal those wounds—to be free within herself
of the person(s) and/or events that hurt her. It is also important to
continue to heal yourself. There is tremendous freedom and power
that comes when you are finally able to forgive. The challenge is to
get to a place where you are ready to let go.

When you do forgive, you free yourself from the past. You
open yourself to what the present and the future have for you. You
deserve this freedom.

Patty, a mom of four, said, "I have a list a mile long of hurts
that I want to heal and people I need to forgive, including myself.
That one is probably the hardest of all. I am stubborn. I know I
am hurting myself the most when I continue to hold on to these
wounds. I want to let go. I want to feel what it is like to have truly
forgiven. It's time to move forward. Praying that I will be shown
how to let go helps. I know I will have a much better life once I do."

A part of Patty wants to forgive herself, as well as others who hurt her in the past. And yet a part of her hangs on. Once you are truly open, you can forgive. *Forgiving the person who has wronged you is more beneficial to you than it is to the person who hurt you.*

We all make mistakes. Children make mistakes. Some are big. Some are small. Mistakes are opportunities to learn. Children want to learn right from wrong. They want to learn how to grow up and be independent, honest, and loving adults. They want a mom who understands that, when they make a mistake, they are not bad. They sometimes make poor choices. They want a mom who will not shame or embarrass them, but will forgive them for their errors and help them make better choices next time. Children want to feel good about themselves.

When children have moms who are forgiving of them and of others, they will most likely grow up to be more forgiving people. They will develop the ability to forgive naturally, because they will know what it feels like when someone forgives them. They, in turn, will be able to forgive more readily—both themselves and others—when they are hurt. Remember, children learn from how you behave, not just from what you say.

Children want moms who model forgiveness and getting on with the good things in life. Sandra Burt and Linda Perlis sum it up well in their book *Raising a Successful Child*: "We can preach and lecture all we want, but to our children, our life is our message."

Forgiveness

Very few moms have told me that they were raised by forgiving parents. Here's what a few of them shared in a parenting class.

Angie said, "I don't ever remember hearing the words 'forgive or let go.' My parents always blamed someone else. Nothing was ever their fault. They are still like that today. Now that I have children, they shame and blame my children for every little thing. My children act out when we are there more than usual. I think it's because my parents blame them so often. Now that they are older, they don't even want to go see them. I don't blame them."

Cindy added, "My mom used to say that she forgave my dad every time he came home drunk or spent money he shouldn't have. It didn't matter to him. He still treated her horribly. I think she acted as if she forgave him because she was so afraid of him."

I have talked to many moms over the years, and I have yet to hear from more than a handful that they ever experienced any kind of genuine forgiveness from their parents. Moreover, most parents are not forgiving of themselves. Listen to Sara's take on her mom: "My mom didn't think she was worthy of forgiving herself. She felt ashamed of her past. Her parents had not approved of her behavior and had never forgiven her. It was when she finally got into recovery that she began the process of forgiving, not only herself, but others. Today, she more readily forgives us kids when we make a mistake. I have also been more open to forgive her for her past. It has really helped our relationship. I wish my grandparents would forgive my mom, but I know they never will."

Annie said, "Every weekend, my parents came home drunk. One of them usually got mad at us kids for no reason and usually ended up hitting us. The next morning, they apologized. The next weekend, the same thing happened again. It never changed. Apologies mean nothing to me. They are just hollow words. I haven't been able to forgive them. I hated them for hitting me."

Janice reflected, "At least your parents apologized. When we had something like that happen, my mom somehow turned it around. I always ended up feeling that I was the bad one. I begged her to please forgive me. She always refused, saying I didn't deserve forgiveness. It was not until I was in my late teens that I realized I hadn't done anything wrong. It was her way of controlling me. We don't get along today. I hope someday she will apologize."

I think most of us would agree that forgiveness is not always easy. It is, however, easier to forgive than to carry around the burdens of resentment and anger. Forgiveness means admitting that what has happened to you is a reality. It's mostly about letting go—completely and permanently—and not snatching those feelings back. Forgiveness mostly happens within yourself.

"Hanging on to resentments is letting someone you despise live rent-free in your head" (author unknown). Just picturing this statement may help you move forward in your process of forgiving.

Letting Go

The following piece of Refrigerator Wisdom is one of my all-time favorites. I don't know who wrote this particular saying, but I have pulled it out of my file many times over the years. I seem to find whatever message I need within these words every single time I read them.

> To let go doesn't mean to stop caring; it means I can't do it for someone else.
> To let go is not to cut myself off; it's the realization that I can't control another.
> To let go is not to enable, but to allow learning from natural consequences.
> To let go is to admit powerlessness, which means the outcome is not in my hands.
> To let go is not to try to change or blame another; it's to make the most of myself.
> To let go is not to care for, but to care about.
> To let go is not to fix, but to be supportive.
> To let go is not to judge, but to allow another to be a human being.

To let go is not to be in the middle arranging all the outcomes,
but to allow others to affect their own outcome.
To let go is not to be protective; it is to permit another
to face reality.
To let go is not to deny, but to accept.
To let go is not to nag, scold, or argue, but instead to search
out my own shortcomings and correct them.
To let go is not to adjust everything to my desires, but to
take each day as it comes and to cherish myself in it.
To let go is not to criticize and regulate anyone, but to try to
become what I dream I can be.
To let go is not to regret the past, but to grow and live
for the future.
To let go is to fear less and love more.
and
To let go and to let God, is to find peace!

You are a valuable and important person. Creating the very best life for you and your children is part of your hopes and dreams. Continuing to carry guilt takes a lot of unnecessary energy.

Picture yourself with a huge bag flung over your shoulder, something like Santa's bag. Yours is not full of gifts, however. Yours is full of past mistakes, guilt, hurts, wrongdoings, shame, disappointments, regrets. Can you imagine how heavy it is to carry all of this around with you every day? Exhausting. Now imagine that you put the bag down and walk away from it. Do you feel lighter? More free? This is how it feels when you forgive and move on.

Forgiving yourself is a gift you can give yourself. When you forgive yourself, you free yourself of past mistakes. You can move forward to create the life you dream of. When you forgive yourself, you also acknowledge that you are no longer a victim. You are truly free to live.

When you forgive another, you benefit far more than the other person. *The longer you put off forgiveness, the longer you remain in the belief that you are a victim.* Yes, someone has angered, offended, or hurt you in some way. But you have been a participant in the process. The sooner you make the decision to forgive, the sooner you can let go and move on. *Your forgiveness is a sign that you are no longer willing to participate in your own victimization.*

While it is sometimes difficult to forgive, it is much less burdensome to forgive (let go of the Santa bag) than to go through each day feeling resentment and bitterness. Many times, the other person is not even aware that you are feeling this way. So who is this hurting the most?

As we said in chapter 4, anger can nearly consume you. It also spreads out to your children and to others in your life. When you forgive, you free yourself of the anger that has not been serving you. You recognize what happened, and you no longer let it run your life.

So what does it mean to forgive? Wayne Dyer tells us, "Forgiveness is the ability to give love away in the most difficult of circumstances." Forgiveness does not mean that what you did was okay, or that what someone did to you was okay. It means that you no longer want or are willing to let past behaviors hold you back from going forward in your life.

It also does not mean that you are willing to be hurt again. By forgiving, you take the steps forward that will help you become stronger and more solid within yourself. You can be proud of who you are. You deserve to be proud of yourself. You are a strong and determined woman!

How to Forgive

In a parenting class, we discussed some of the different ways you can forgive.

PRAYER

Amber said, "I pray. I just keep on praying until I feel an actual release. I wake up one morning, and I realize that I am not so angry. I continue to pray. Over a period of time, the anger and the hurt feelings seem to go away. I am not filled with rage anymore."

A classmate asked her, "What do you pray?"

"I pray that I will be helped to forgive. That I will be free of the person and or the thing that hurt me. I pray to be strong and loving. I pray to be free of the past."

Most of the moms in the class agreed that prayer is a very important part of their forgiving process. Some shared that, sometimes, all they know to do is to say the Serenity Prayer (attributed to Reinhold Niebuhr) over and over until the feelings subside.

> God, grant me the serenity to accept the things
>   I cannot change.
> The courage to change the things I can.
> And the wisdom to know the difference.

WRITING

Lisa said, "I write. I used to write about what had happened. Now, I write my feelings. They change from day to day. It doesn't help me to write the same thing over and over. I am moving toward being free of this. After I've written for a while, I write a prayer, asking to help me forgive. I usually feel better and end up saying a prayer also asking for help. I carry a little notebook with me so that, whenever I feel the need to write and have a few minutes, I find a spot and journal."

FORGIVING IN PERSON

Sometimes you can go to a person and tell them that, even though they have hurt you, you forgive them. Remember, this is more for you than for them. Putting down the burden gives you a lighter load. How the other person chooses to respond or not respond does not affect you. Your part is to forgive and set yourself free. At other times, you cannot talk to the person who hurt you. You can, however, ask a close friend, a sponsor, or a therapist to sit with you and allow you to say everything that you need to say, as if the other person were sitting in front of you. Again, this frees you.

AFFIRMATIONS

"I use affirmations," said Marie. "I speak the words as though the forgiving has already occurred. The more I say them, the stronger I feel. I really can forgive the past. I need to forgive myself as well as others."

Affirmations tell your mind how you want something to be by speaking the words as though it already is. Your mind takes you literally. At the end of each chapter, I've given you affirmations. I encourage you to say them and write them over and over. They are more powerful than you may realize.

Here are a few examples of affirmations that are specifically for forgiveness.

I forgive myself for past mistakes.

I let go of my need to be a victim.

I forgive others that have hurt me in the past. I am now free to truly live my life.

HAVE A BONFIRE

Sometimes creating a ritual can help you forgive. Gather up a piece of writing, or several of your writings, that you have done about this particular person or event and toss them into your fireplace, barbeque pit, or bonfire. As you watch them burn, pray that the person is now forgiven and that you are free.

Many years ago, a friend invited me to a "Letting Go" ritual at the beach. As each person arrived, we were given pieces of paper and a pen and told to find a quiet place and write anything that we would like to forgive and let go of that evening. People were quiet and reflective. After a period of time, my friend called everyone back.

A fire had been built. One by one, each person had the option to share what they had written or not. When everyone was ready, we tossed our papers into the fire. Some cried when it was their turn. Some whooped and hollered as they watched their papers burn. Others remained quiet, just staring at the fire. Once everyone had finished, we shared prayers of gratitude for the lightness and freedom that we had just received.

Sometimes you need to do your forgiving privately. Sometimes, it is helpful to have someone else there. There are many other ways to forgive. The how is not so important. Taking the steps to forgive is what matters most.

Teaching Your Children to Forgive

When you forgive, you free yourself and move forward with your life. When you do this, you teach your children that they do not have to carry the burdens of the past. Children tend to be very forgiving. I am often touched to be with a mother when she humbly asks her child for forgiveness. Many times, especially with young children, they have already forgiven their moms. Young children have a natural acceptance of their moms.

Teens and young adults don't always forgive so readily. They need time to work through their own feelings. Maybe you have not always stuck to your word, or maybe, because of your actions, your children were taken away from you. They need to rebuild their trust in you. This takes you showing them, over a period of time, that you are staying in your recovery. I understand that, once you are clean and sober, you may want them to forget and forgive the past. To see you as you are today. Be patient with them. Give them the time they need. We all heal in our own way and our own time. If you demonstrate patience and understanding of their process and remain solid in your recovery, the odds are better that they will come around.

Doug, age twenty-two, reflected, "My mom was an alcoholic ever since I can remember. Now she's been in recovery two years and keeps begging me to trust her that she will never drink again. I don't know if she will or won't. That's not even so much why I can't forgive her. It's all of the things that happened to me while I was growing up that I can't forgive. If she had been a mom like she was supposed to be, I wouldn't have had to be moved from relative to relative. I think I went to ten different schools. Every time I began to adjust, something would happen and I'd be moved again. It was hard. I was jealous of my friends who had a reliable parent. I suffered for twenty years; she can wait for me now."

Doug shared his hurt and anger well. He had legitimate reasons to feel the way he did. I hope, for his own sake, that he will not carry this for another twenty years.

Anna shared a picture she had drawn. It was of a big house. There were lots of windows and doors. The front door was wide open. The inside of the house was black. Sitting in the corner was a little girl, hiding, and a baby. The little girl was very scared and had tears coming down her cheeks. The baby was asleep on the floor. I asked Anna to tell me about her picture.

"This was my house. My mom used to drink and do drugs. She used to get really mean and mad at us kids. Eventually, she'd storm out the door screaming that she hated us brats and saying she was never coming back. I was nine years old the first time it happened. I was so afraid that someone was going to come in and take us. I got my baby brother and sat in the corner in the dark, hoping we would not get kidnapped. I didn't know what to do or if she would ever come back."

Anna, now fourteen, cried as she shared this memory. "This happened many times before my mom got into recovery. My brother and I were in foster homes for a long time. My mom fought to get us back. I was afraid to go back with her. Eventually, we did move back in with her. She doesn't storm out or call us names anymore. She is a much better mom now that she is in recovery. She and I go to therapy together. It is helping us, because I get to tell her how it was for me. She cries sometimes, but she doesn't yell at me. I don't yet completely trust her or forgive her. I want to forgive her. I know I will if things keep going as they have been. The therapist says that I can have all the time I need to forgive. My mom tells me that too."

Mistakes

Most parents of today were raised to think and feel that making a mistake was a bad thing. Usually guilt, blame, and shame were a part of the reprimand, coming just before being spanked or grounded, or given some other punishment. I asked the class how it was for them as children when they made a mistake.

Amanda offered, "By kindergarten, I was already very sneaky. I had learned that, when I did anything at all wrong, if I hid the mistake, I didn't get in trouble."

"'Only stupid kids make such dumb mistakes. How can you be so stupid?' That's what I always heard," said Bethany. "No matter what I did wrong, I was punished. The punishment depended on whether Mom and Dad were in good or bad moods. It had nothing to do with what I had done wrong. That never made sense to me. Mistakes were definitely something bad. When we made one, we were bad."

Well, here's some good news for you and your children. We all make mistakes. Children, parents, grandparents, aunts, uncles, even teachers and doctors make mistakes. That doesn't make us bad or stupid. Fortunately, today's children can be raised with a healthier belief about mistakes. I am particularly fond of the saying, "There are no accidents or mistakes, only opportunities for growth and discovery," and use it often.

My five-year-old granddaughter, Bailey, talks about mistakes with such confidence. She was with me one day when I dropped a crystal vase. I gasped and then began cleaning it up. I knew she was watching me to see if I was going to be mad or not.

She walked over to me and softly said, "It was a mistake, Mimi. It's okay to make mistakes, huh Mimi? I'll hold the dustpan." She helped me clean it up. A little while later, she said, "Mimi, what do you think you could have done so it wouldn't have fallen out of your hands?"

I almost fell on the floor. Here's this five-year-old walking me through precisely what we had been working through in our group about mistakes.

Here's what Bailey thinks about mistakes:

1. They happen. It's okay.

2. Tell the truth that you made the mistake. Don't blame your brother or someone else.

3. If you break something, clean it up. If you do something mean, admit it and say you are sorry.

4. After it's all over, think or talk about how you can do it differently next time.

Bailey and I decided that I had too many things in my hands at once. Next time, I won't try to carry so many things, and I probably won't drop anything. There was no guilt, or shame, or blaming. No one was mad. I loved seeing how she handled this. I feel confident that, when she grows up, she will have a more healthy understanding of the fact that it's okay to make a mistake. The key is to learn from the mistake, take any responsibility that is yours, and move on.

This is certainly different from what I experienced many times as a child. When I was about ten, my sister and I were supposed to be doing the dishes, and we got into a little soap fight. In the moments of laughter, my sister accidentally dropped a crystal pitcher that my mom had had forever. My mom's face and body language immediately told us that we had done something very wrong. She wouldn't even speak to us or look at us. She just began to cry, motioned for us to get out of the way, and cleaned it up. We kept offering to help, but she ignored us. In fact, she didn't talk to us for a few days. That was one of her ways of punishing us. We felt sorry for breaking the pitcher and told her so many times. I remember feeling helpless because my mom would not forgive us. We knew it was an accident, and yet both of us were filled with guilt and shame.

Nothing more was said about it until, one holiday about fifteen years later, in front of everyone at the table, our mom began telling the story of who had given her the pitcher and how much it had meant to her. She then went on to share how we had broken it because we were being careless. Once again, she piled on another layer of guilt and shame about something that had happened fifteen years before. And along with the guilt and shame, she embarrassed both of us. We felt ambushed. Where was this coming from? Needless to say, we were surprised, almost beyond words, that she chose this occasion to bring it up. I doubt that she ever did forgive us.

I learned some valuable lessons from this experience. When something like this happens, address it with your children once you are calmed down. It would have been so much more helpful if she had sat down with us and talked about how the mistake could have been prevented. Please do not carry around something your children did that made you mad. Deal with it in the present and move forward. In other words, please don't wait fifteen years to shame and embarrass your children for something they did or didn't do all those years ago.

JOURNALING ACTIVITY

1. Write your recollections of forgiveness in your family when you were a child.

2. Choose a few of the sentences in the "Letting Go" poem that you especially like or are drawn to. Write how they touch you.

3. Do you have a "Santa's bag"? Is it full of past mistakes, hurts, shame, regret? If it is, dump them out. What would you fill the bag with now?

4. What can you do to help yourself get to a place of forgiveness?

5. Is it harder to forgive yourself or someone else? Why?

6. Who do you need to forgive? Make a list if you need to. What do you need to do to forgive them? How are you going to forgive them?

GEMS FOR YOUR POCKET

When I forgive, I benefit myself far more than the other person.

To let go is to fear less and love more.

Everyone makes mistakes.

Mistakes are opportunities to learn.

There is no need to shame or blame anyone when a mistake happens.

Children learn by how you behave as much or more than by what you say.

AFFIRMATIONS

I forgive myself and others.

I am free of the past.

I am open to give and receive goodness in my life.

I am proud of who I am.

I learn from my mistakes.

I give my children the understanding and time that they need to heal.

I am patient and kind.

I am strong in my recovery.

I am enough.

CHAPTER 6

Building Healthy Self-Esteem

> You really have to look inside yourself and find your own inner strength, and say, "I'm proud of what I am and who I am, and I'm just going to be myself."
>
> —*Mariah Carey*

Every mom wants to remain strong in her recovery. You want to let go of parts of the past as you create the life you deserve. Feeling good about yourself and accepting yourself exactly as you are are things every mom wants. This may be a challenge, because you do not yet feel deserving. Take the strength and determination within you and begin building your confidence. As it builds, your self-esteem builds. As your esteem grows, you will have more confidence to do what is important to you—going back to school, finding a new job, or a safe and secure place to live. Whatever it is, with healthy self-esteem, you can move forward.

Yes, of course, you will make mistakes along the way. The beauty of having healthy self-esteem is that you can pick yourself up and try again. Every mom wants to succeed. Every day that you remain in your recovery is a success. Be proud of yourself for that alone. Build your self-esteem from there. Anytime you forget, come back to this page and read these words: *You are a strong and determined woman. You deserve a full and joyful life. Your confidence builds every day.*

All children want to know that they are loved and lovable. Feeling loved and knowing they matter is important to children. Having healthy self-esteem is not a function of wealth, education, social class, a two-parent home, or their parents' jobs or careers. It is a function of the quality of the relationships that occur over the years between you, your child, and other important people in your child's life.

Many times, parents take for granted that their children know that they are loved. This is not always the case. Maybe the parents' words and actions do not convey love to the child. There is a difference between being loved and feeling loved. It is vitally important that, in addition to being loved, your child also feels loved.

Alex, age twelve, shared, "I know my mom loves me. She shows up at my soccer games. She helps me with my homework without getting mad. She listens to me. Sometimes, when I'm upset, she hugs me and doesn't say a word. I feel loved. My dad, on the other hand, says he loves me. He buys me anything I want when I see him. The problem is, most of the time, he doesn't show up for our visit. I don't think he really loves me or he would try harder. He buys me stuff to make himself feel less guilty and acts as if he's being a good dad. But he's not. I see right through him. I wish my dad were like my friends' dads. They do things with their kids. They show up at their ball games. I've never had any of that with my dad."

The more Alex shared, the sadder he became. Children learn the truth about each of their parents at a very young age.

Children want to be accepted and taken care of, and to know that their moms will do anything to keep them safe. They want to know that, if anything happens to them, their mom will be sad and miss them. They feel good about who they are because they know they are important.

Looking Back so you can Move forward

Your parents, as well as your entire family, greatly influenced how you feel about yourself today. You were affected by your own parents' self-esteem. How did they appear to feel about themselves? People with healthy self-esteem are confident and believe in themselves. They value their health and take good care of their bodies. Does this sound like your parents?

Other adults, like day-care providers, aunts, uncles, and teachers, can also be very influential in increasing or decreasing a person's self-esteem. Did you have one special person who always encouraged you? Someone you knew believed in you? Or did you have someone who put you down and conveyed that you would never be a success? Adult role models are powerful.

No one likes to be compared to someone else. If you had siblings, you most likely remember what it felt like when your parents compared you to them. "Why can't you get good grades like your sister?" "Sit up and eat your dinner quietly like your brother." "Look at this mess! Why can't you keep your room clean like your sister?" Statements like these chip away at a child's self-esteem. Children may begin to feel that they are not good enough no matter what they do. So why try?

Heather shared her experience: "To this day, my mom still tells me I should be more like my sister. She's finished college and has a job. I've never felt good enough or smart enough. So why try? I've heard this from her for as long as I can remember. Maybe that's why I never really tried very hard in school."

Claire offered, "When I was eleven, I remember my dad telling me, 'You're just like your mother. You'll never amount to anything. You'll have a bunch of kids. You won't be able to take care of them.' I believed him. He was my dad. As I continue in my recovery, my self-esteem is increasing. It's taking a lot of work to let go of the old beliefs."

April added, "I guess I was lucky. My fourth-grade teacher was glad to see me every single morning. I remember feeling so happy because she smiled at me. She always told me that I was talented in art and could do anything I wanted. She was the first and only adult in my life that talked with me about one day going to college and becoming a teacher like her, or a doctor, or an artist, or whatever I wanted to be. I believed her."

Children are like sponges. They soak up nearly everything they see, hear, and feel. How fortunate April was to have had this teacher to give her encouragement and to open her eyes to all of the possibilities for her life.

April continued, "That's probably one of the reasons that I've had the courage to begin taking some art classes at the JC. I will never forget that teacher. I will never forget how I felt that one year because she made me feel special. I was important. I cannot even imagine what it would have been like to have had a mom who believed in me like that."

Justine said, "My self-esteem began building bit by bit once I went into recovery. I felt proud of myself for taking the step. Every time I achieve even the smallest goal, I feel proud. I feel better about myself. I know I still have a lot of guilt and shame, but I'm getting there. I'm at least going in the right direction."

The relationships and experiences that you have had up until now have all contributed to your self-esteem—for better or worse. If you were fortunate enough to have loving parents and to grow up in a stable environment, your self-esteem may be solid. If you had abusive parents and lived in an unstable environment, your self-esteem may not yet be where you want or deserve it to be. And it's not only your parents who helped shape you. Your extended family, your neighbors and friends, how you performed in school— all these things influenced how you feel about yourself today.

Both external and internal sources impact your self-esteem. As a child, you were judged by the area you lived in, the kind of clothes you wore, what kind of a job your parents had, even what kind of car they drove. These are the external sources. As an adult, you know this is not really who you are. And yet, because of others' opinions and beliefs about things like this, as a child you either felt proud and superior or ashamed and inferior.

The way you were disciplined may also have had an adverse effect on your self-esteem. In chapter 1, we talked about the three styles of discipline. If you had authoritarian parents who abused you with physical and verbal punishments, your self-esteem was most likely affected adversely. You were taught to believe that you were somehow bad if your parents had to punish you in the ways they did. Today, you know it was not because you were bad. They did not have appropriate parenting skills to guide you. As a child, you took their treatment of you personally and internalized it. These internal feelings and beliefs are largely responsible for your level of self-esteem.

what is Healthy self-esteem?

In a parenting class, I once wrote on the board: How do people with healthy self-esteem see themselves? Here's the list the group came up with:

Confident

Self-assured

Able to set and accomplish goals

Loved unconditionally

Independent

Able to make decisions

Accepted by others

Accepting of others

Valued

Important in the community and society in general

Secure in who they are and what they say and do

Involved in positive relationships

Proud

Healthy self-esteem includes all of the above. Self-esteem is the overall feeling you have about yourself. It's more than what shows on the outside—more than your physical appearance, the way you talk and act, your education or career. *Healthy self-esteem is a strong but quiet sense of self-respect. A knowingness that you are an important and valuable being just as you are.*

When you have healthy self-esteem, you don't need to impress others. You already know you have value. Self-esteem begins in early infancy. When babies cry, if they are picked up and gently soothed, they begin to feel safe and secure. They feel loved. When the adults in their lives respond to their smiles and talk to them lovingly, their self-esteem grows. The foundation for healthy self-esteem is being laid.

As babies grow, if they feel loved and cared for by the adults in their lives, they feel they are valued and important. These beliefs help bring them to healthy self-esteem. On the other hand, if they are ignored or punished as a way of discipline, their self-esteem will not flourish. Punishment diminishes, rather than builds, self-esteem.

While self-esteem starts at a young age, it is never too late to begin building it in yourself or your children. If your children were not with you in the early years and now you only see them on occasion, make sure that whatever time you are together is a positive experience for you and for them. I do not mean that you should spend the time buying them things or taking them places. Use the time to be *present* with them. Let them know that you accept them just as they are. Encourage them to do their best. Show them that you believe in them. Enjoy them. Appreciate them and the time you spend together.

Here's how a few moms described what they want their self-esteem to look one year from now.

Tisch said, "I am confident. Even when I fail at something, I know that I am not a loser or a bad person. I know I need to try it again. Maybe another way. I am proud of myself, both in my recovery and as a mom. I respect myself much more now."

Lynn added, "One time a woman at my church said she had fallen in love with herself. I thought that was weird. Now I know what she was talking about. Until I learn to love and appreciate myself for exactly who I am, how can I ever give that to anyone else? No wonder my relationships weren't working. I am proud of myself for taking responsibility for my past mistakes and doing what it takes to clean them up. I feel so much better about myself now. When I have an argument with someone, I'm able to take responsibility for my part and be accountable."

Heather agreed. "For me, it's all of the above, as well as the fact that I am finally independent. I can take care of myself. I have a steady job. I'm capable of supporting me and my kids. Once I got the job, I began making other decisions about our lives. It's getting better. My kids are beginning to trust me more that I will take care of them. They seem more relaxed now and even help out sometimes."

Pat chimed in, "For twenty-four years, I lied, stole, manipulated, did whatever I had to do to get what I wanted. I felt like the lowest person on the face of the Earth. I didn't care. Once I began my recovery, I admitted that I didn't like me at all. I was such a loser. Fortunately, day by day, I learned to be honest, not only with myself, but with my counselor. That was a turning point for me. I still have work to do. Recovery is not easy. I am proud that I can say that I am an honest person today. I am honest about my past, as well as about whatever comes my way each day. This is what has most helped my self-esteem."

Encouragement and Praise

Praise is giving your children an opinion or judgment. Encouragement is letting your children know you believe in them. My five-year-old granddaughter was a flower girl at her aunt's wedding. I noticed many people telling her, "You are so cute. What a good job you did." She just kind of looked at them with a blank expression and ended the encounter. What they didn't know was that she did not feel cute because her dress was scratchy. She did not feel proud of the way she walked down the aisle. While they meant to compliment her, they really only confused her. Actually, they irritated her.

That was empty—though well-meant—praise. Encouragement is something different. Encouragement is being right there to support your children—no matter what. Sometimes simply repeating what a child is saying can be encouraging. This is what was most helpful to our little flower girl in the minutes preceding the wedding. Here's one of the conversations we had that day.

"I have never been a flower girl before. Have you?" she asked.

"I know," I replied. "This is your first time being in a wedding. And no, I have never been a flower girl."

"I feel nervous," she admitted.

"Yes. You do feel nervous," I acknowledged.

"I have butterflies."

"You do have butterflies!"

"Do you think I can do my job?" she asked nervously.

Without hesitating, I said: "I do. Bailey, I know you can do your job!"

It might have been tempting to try to talk her out of her feelings, but that would not have helped her. As I just calmly repeated back to her what she was telling me, she calmed herself. Her confidence built enough for her to walk down the aisle tossing the rose petals.

Simply restating what someone says to you is called reflective listening. It may feel awkward and phony at first. But as you see your child responding in a positive way, you will discover what a useful tool it is. And reflective listening is not just for children. It is a communication tool that can be used with anyone.

Here's how my conversation with Bailey might have gone without reflective listening.

"I have never been a flower girl before. Have you?"

"No I haven't. But it's no big deal. You'll do fine."

"I feel nervous."

"Oh Bailey," I say, slightly irritated, "There's nothing to be nervous about. You're fine."

"I have butterflies," she admits.

"You're being ridiculous now," I answer, even more irritated.

"Do you think I can do my job?" she asks.

"Oh Bailey," I snap back, frustrated and minimizing her nervousness. "It's not a job. All you have to do is walk down the aisle, sprinkling the petals. Just think of how Gigi must be feeling right now. She's the bride. She's the one who should be scared, not you."

Do you see and hear the difference in the two scenarios? Which conversation would you like to have if you were Bailey? We need to remember: *Children need to be seen and heard.* Your words to them can make a lasting impression. Your words can build or decrease their confidence.

A week after the wedding, Bailey and I had another conversation.

"Do you remember the wedding?" she asked. "I had never been a flower girl before."

"Yes," I replied. "I remember the wedding. It was your very first time to be a flower girl."

"I was nervous," she giggled. "That's why I didn't smile going down that path. I was thinking about my job. I had so many rose petals to throw. I wanted to do it right for Gigi."

"You were nervous," I acknowledged. "You were serious because you were thinking so hard about the rose petals."

"I think I did a good job," she said, looking at me hopefully. "Next time I'm the flower girl, I will know exactly how to do it. I won't be nervous."

I just smiled and gave her a hug. We went on about our day.

I hope that you can see, from this simple example, how my encouragement was much more helpful to her than empty praise would have been. Even though she was nervous, she succeeded. *When we have any kind of success, our self-esteem goes up.*

I must admit that I was a little surprised that Bailey came around to feeling that she had had such a positive experience as flower girl. On the day of the wedding, I don't think any of us thought she would have a wonderful memory about being in Gigi's wedding. Children are so brave and resilient. With lots of love, acceptance, encouragement, and support, they sure can succeed.

is There such a Thing as Too Much Praise?

Do you believe that you should praise your child as much as possible? It sounds like a good idea. I imagine that you would have loved to have been praised more when you were a child. I understand that.

Praise that is genuine and heartfelt is good for your child. But some parents praise too much and too often. Let's look at what can happen when you praise too much. If you praise your children for everything they do, by the time they are three, or four, or five, they may not only expect praise, they may rely on it. If you don't praise them, they may think they have failed. They may end up thinking, "Something is wrong because mom is not telling me that I did a good job."

Have you ever heard your child ask, while coloring a picture, "Mommy, is this right? Is this good? Am I doing good?" Children may go on and on like this until you finally comment just to shut them up. They have learned to depend on your judgment, your opinion of their project, instead of simply enjoying the coloring. They are giving away a part of their power that you really don't want to take from them.

Some moms find themselves praising too much or too often. You may want to make up for the time, while in your addiction, when you were not there for your child. *Children are unlikely to build healthy self-esteem when they are praised too much.* They see right through your words. They may lose trust in any person who heaps on praise indiscriminately. They begin to doubt the words, not knowing what to believe and what not to believe. Instead of becoming more independent as they get older, they become more dependent on you.

Encouragement and praise are not the same. If we praise too much, we take away from the child's experience. For example, your child comes home with a "good" report card. Instead of saying, "I am so proud of you. You are the smartest kid I know." Try saying, "You must be proud of yourself. Your grades show that you have worked very hard." This allows children to feel proud of their accomplishment regardless of how you feel.

Imagine you are in an art class. You've been working on a painting for many weeks. I come walking in and say, "What a beautiful painting. I really like it. You are certainly the most talented artist in this class." What does that feel like? You may think, "What's so beautiful about it? I know that I am not the best artist in the class." Maybe you are not yet satisfied with the painting, but, because I approve, you dismiss your own thoughts and take on mine. But what if I walk in and say, "Tell me how you're doing with this painting?" My opinions or judgments are not involved. This gives you the opportunity to share your thoughts and feelings about your work. After all, it is yours, not mine.

When you praise children too much, they miss out on opportunities to learn what they like and don't like. They miss out on learning to make their own decisions. Think of a time when you did something you were proud of. Did you get to feel how it felt? Or did someone else say or do something that took your feelings of accomplishment away?

Nicole shared this: "When I was ten, I had made my first dress with a zipper. My mom said, 'I am really proud of you. I like the dress. You listened and you did everything the way I told you.' It felt like mom's dress then. Because I did everything the way she said, it felt like it was her sewing project, not mine."

Kelly added, "I was a very good student. I worked hard to get good grades. I will never forget one semester when I came home with a report card that was all As and one A-minus. I was so excited to show it to my mom. She took one look at it and said, 'What happened here? Why the A-minus? How do you expect to get into college if you are getting A-minuses?' I felt so ashamed, and to this day, I feel like a failure. I've been afraid to go back to school. Not only was I a failure, but I knew I had let my mom down."

Every year, when you receive a chip for another year of your recovery, are you proud of yourself? While it is nice to hear the clapping and cheering, would it be okay if no one else were there but you? Take moments like that and feel your own success. You are the one succeeding! These very feelings are what lead you to know that you are a lovable and worthwhile person. As your awareness increases, so does your self-esteem.

When my daughter Andrea was a sophomore in high school, she made up her mind that she was going to be a foreign-exchange student the following year. She wanted to study in Australia. She began getting the information and applications she needed to pursue her goal. One day, full of excitement and belief in her dream, she told her grandfather of her plan. He listened and then said, "Go ahead and apply, but you probably won't get accepted, so don't get too excited about it." She was crushed—mad and very sad. Recently, when she was recollecting this memory, she said, "He was probably trying to protect me, but I felt shattered and deflated." As a teen, she allowed his disbelief in her plan to take away her enthusiasm temporarily. Fortunately, she is a very determined young woman and continued in her planning.

By the way, he was at the airport when she boarded the plane for her year in Australia!

wise women and Gremlins

We all have within us a voice that is wise. I call mine my "Wise Woman" voice. You can use that name if you like. Others call it their intuition, their gut feeling, their inner instinct. Do you sometimes experience a knowingness about something? A gut feeling?

Maybe you have the opportunity to change jobs. Even though a part of you may really want a new job, there is this quiet, consistent, calm feeling that keeps telling you this is not the time for you to make the change. Maybe you trust that voice enough to turn down the job. Soon, it becomes clear why your Wise Woman voice (your intuition) encouraged you to stay where you are for now. Or you decide not to pay attention, and you go ahead and change jobs. Two months later, the company closes, and you are out of work. Maybe your intuition was trying to forewarn you.

Have you ever kept thinking about calling a friend that you haven't seen for a long time? You walk into the grocery store and there is that very friend. Though it may seem a little strange, intuitiveness is not really a mystery. It is a deeper level of perception that each person is given. The more you acknowledge and pay attention to it, the more skilled you become with your intuition.

Many times, we choose not to pay attention to our inner voices. We don't encourage them out of the mistaken belief that we humans really don't have this gift of knowingness. Those of us who do practice using and trusting our intuition find it more and more helpful. It has helped me to have a deeper understanding of our world.

We also have an inner voice that I call "the Gremlin." It's that voice that sometimes speaks loudly and sometimes just keeps on chattering. It likes to have your power. It's the voice that judges and criticizes you about the choices you make and the way you are leading your life. Again, you can call this inner voice your Gremlin if you like, or maybe you already have a name that fits. Many use words like judge, critic, dad voice, mom voice, boss. Find what works for you.

Do you ever hear a voice saying, "You'll never amount to anything," or "You don't deserve to have that new car," or "You'll never finish that class. So why start?" Sound familiar? If you give your Gremlin your power, it will happily take, not only your power, but your self-esteem too.

You know that voice of doubt that continues to remind you of your past, your mistakes, your vulnerabilities, your self-imposed limitations? That too, is ol' Gremlin. Begin paying attention when those negative thoughts come into your head. Every time they appear, all you need do is let your Gremlin know that you have no time for or interest in the messages. It's time to exit. Your Gremlin is used to hanging out with you. Without realizing it, you have given power to the voice. The good news is that you have the power to change it. If your Gremlin is persistent—and it most likely will be—stay in your power, repeating your request for it to leave and stay away. Do this for as long as it takes.

As a child and through your addiction, you were told by others that you wouldn't accomplish anything. Part of you believed it. Maybe you still do. Now that you are in recovery, your confidence is building. *You can accomplish absolutely anything you desire.* If you discipline yourself to be consistent in the belief that you are a good person and can create the life you want, your doubt will eventually fade.

Each time your Gremlin appears and you make your request, you will be one step closer to being free. As you free yourself of ol' Gremlin, there will be more opportunity for your Wise Woman to assist you.

Building Your Self-esteem

Here are some simple ways to help build your own self-esteem.

STOP COMPARING

No one likes to be compared. You didn't like or benefit from being compared to siblings as a child. So, why do you sometimes compare yourself to others?

"She's much smarter than I am. I could never pass that class."

"Her car is like new. Mine's a heap."

"Her parents support her. Why can't mine?'

Sound familiar? How many times do you, without even realizing it, think how much better off you would be if you had someone else's life—or at least parts of it? The sentences above are full of put-downs. When you catch yourself making these kinds of comparisons, stop. When you catch yourself comparing your children, stop.

STOP THE PUT-DOWNS

Your brain takes you literally. Every time you put yourself down, you sabotage your own self-esteem. You also influence how others feel about you. If you repeatedly say, "I am so dumb. I could never do that," you not only begin to believe it, you also encourage others to see you as someone who is not very smart. Having just read about the Gremlin and the Wise Woman, who do you think is chattering in your head when you make statements like these? Of course, it's ol' Gremlin just trying to keep you down. I believe that, once your

Gremlin is gone, your Wise Woman will quietly reassure you that you can do whatever you want in this world. You are a bright and healthy woman. You are capable—and you are deserving.

FELLOWSHIP AND COMMUNITY

Those of you who know me have most likely heard me say more than once, "It takes a whole village to raise a child." It's an old African proverb. It's so true. It does take a village. The responsibility is on us, as parents, to create a village that is loving, safe, and secure. I use the word "village," but you may call it your community, your support system, your fellowship, or something else.

The people who are a part of your life influence your thoughts and behaviors. Take note of who in your life supports you. Who gives you encouragement? These are the people you want to build relationships with. When you are with them, you feel good about yourself. You feel encouraged and hopeful. Your self-esteem builds.

Who in your life is negative? When you are with them, you find yourself being negative. There may be more drama, more chaos, more gossip. When you share something you are excited about, they immediately put down your idea. Maybe you've decided you want to go back and finish school. It feels right for you. You are excited. You want to share your plan. When you do, someone immediately gives you all the reasons why it isn't a good idea and won't work. Until you are strong within your own self, you may buy into that person's negativity.

Continue to fill your village with people who are positive—people who, like you, want to continue to move forward with their lives. You will soon notice that you have no time, energy, or desire for negative people. Remember the stories that April and Heather shared. As children, they were like sponges, soaking up everything they were told—both positive and negative. Those influences have stayed with them for years. Fill your life with those who have loving hearts and values congruent to yours. As you support and encourage one another, your self-esteem—and theirs—will grow.

Building Your Child's Self-esteem

Remember that your children are learning as much or more from how you behave as from what comes out of your mouth. As you build your self-esteem, you model confidence, self-respect, honesty, and accountability.

Your children want to like themselves. They want to be valued by you and others. With healthy self-esteem, you are more present with your children. Less critical. More accepting. More encouraging. You are giving them the experiences that you didn't have as a child. Can you imagine how it will be for them someday when they are parents—parents who received respect, unconditional love, and encouragement as children? I imagine they will have healthy self-esteem.

Below are some simple ways that you can help build your child's esteem.

1. **Be a role model.** Remember that you are most likely the most influential person in their lives. As they watch you build your own self-esteem, they will be more likely to follow your lead.

2. **Be present.** Everyone wants and needs to be heard. Find times every day when you simply sit and really listen, without judgment or advice, to what they have to say. They will feel they are important to you.

3. **Be respectful.** Treat yourself and your children respectfully. Yelling and threatening is not being respectful. Put-downs are not respectful. Treat your children as you like to be treated. The more respected they feel, the more their self-esteem can build.

4. **Discover what they enjoy.** What are your children's strengths? Find ways for them to experience these activities. If they enjoy sports, find a community soccer, basketball, or baseball team. For a creative child, find art classes, or maybe a drama class. *It's important that you allow your children to do what they enjoy, not make them do what you wish they enjoyed.* For example, if you like music and dance, you may want your children to like it as well. However, when you put them in a dance class, they're miserable. Don't put your likes and dislikes onto your children. Allow them to do what they enjoy. Their confidence and how they feel about themselves will flourish.

5. **Put their needs first.** It's also important to know if your children are team players or enjoy individual sports. One thirteen-year-old told how his mom felt team sports were absolutely the only way to go. "I don't like team sports, like soccer," he said. "I like diving and skiing. We fight all the time about this. Why won't she let me do the things I like? I am a much better diver than I am a soccer player." This mom is putting her wants and needs before her child's.

6. **Make one-on-one quality time.** Convey to your children the message that they are special. Quality time does not mean that you take them to the store and buy them something. Quality time is when you turn off your cell phone, put down your book, get rid of any distractions, and be present with your child. It doesn't matter if you are folding clothes,

pulling weeds, or taking a walk. What matters is that they know that they have your undivided attention. You are connected. This may very well be what is missing most for many children of today.

7. **Give age-appropriate chores.** It's part of being a family. While they may grumble, your children will also feel good about themselves as they accomplish their tasks. Children feel good about themselves when they are helpful and take some responsibility. Frequently, it is the way you present your expectations that influences how your children feel about chores.

8. **Don't compare.** Look for the individual strengths in each of your children and accentuate them. Again, *no one likes being compared to another.*

9. **Offer age-appropriate choices.** When you give your children the opportunity to make choices, they feel good about themselves. For example you may say, "You can take your shower tonight or in the morning," or, for a younger child, "Do you want to have grilled cheese or tuna for lunch?" This allows them to feel that they have some power. It also helps them learn to think for themselves and make choices. It is an early part of teaching responsibility to your child.

10. **Give them encouragement.** Encourage your children to try something new—something that they want to accomplish but are hesitant to attempt. Let them know you are there for them. You believe in them. They will gain more confidence once they give it a try.

11. **Acknowledge their feelings.** Your children want to be seen and understood. When they are sad, let them know that you see their sadness. They don't necessarily want you to fix it.

Nor is it the time to ask them a lot of questions. They simply want you to know how they feel. I imagine you may already know what your children need when they are sad. Do they need a hug? To be left alone? If you don't know, gently ask them. They may be able to tell you. If not, trust your intuition to know what they need at that moment. It is important to remember that each of your children may need something different at these times. For example, when my son was sad, he wanted to be left alone for a little while. When my daughter was sad, she wanted me right there, holding her.

12. **Set realistic expectations.** Realistic expectations give children a sense of control, of age-appropriate power. As their self-control builds, so does their self-esteem.

13. **Catch them being good.** As parents, we tend to point out when our children are doing something wrong. Children like to hear positive comments from you. If you watch, you will discover that they do many things right every day. For example, when they do happen to play nicely with their sister, simply say, "Thank you for playing so well with the baby. She sure loves you." *A positive statement encourages children to want to continue that behavior.*

Maintaining Healthy Self-esteem

Neither you nor your child acquires self-esteem all at once. It continues to grow or diminish, depending on the people around you and your life experiences. A child may feel more confident at home and with familiar people. However, when that child goes to school, that confidence may fade when confronted with a new teacher and new peers. Children want to be accepted and liked by their classmates. However, for most children, one day they may be liked and the next day not. As a mom, you can continue to re-assure your children that you understand and accept them even when others do not.

Your children need to know that life has its ups and downs. A person with healthy self-esteem learns to ride it out. Even when circumstances are uncomfortable or hard, they still need to know they are good people and will figure out what they need to do.

Let's say you've worked at your job for years. There are changes within the business, and you are laid off. A person with healthy self-esteem may initially take it personally, thinking they have done something wrong. But they will soon realize that they are a capable employee and begin looking for a new job.

Jackie, mom of two sons, recently shared this with me: "I have been making sure that I stop and listen to my children every evening. Sometimes, it's at bedtime. We share what was the best and the hardest part of the day. This way we are covering both the listening and the talking. Even if one of us has had a rough day, we end it on a happy note."

I believe that all children not only need but deserve to hear two things at the end of every day: "I love you," and "Tomorrow is a new day." Some days are just plain challenging for both you and your children—from early morning until your heads hit the pillow that night. Your children deserve to go to sleep being reminded that they are loved no matter what. Tomorrow you will all try again.

Helen added, "I am amazed that once I started catching them being good instead of bad, life at home got better. There's actually less fighting now. It's hard for the older two that we have a new baby. When I ask them to get me a blanket or something for the baby, they happily run and get it. I can tell they are proud of themselves. I've learned to give them a big smile and a hug right then. They don't feel so left out."

Stephanie reflected, "I used to be a real athlete. I loved it. I remember how confident I felt during those years. Recently, I really wanted to be in a marathon, but was so scared. I had lost my confidence. It was actually my seventeen-year-old daughter who encouraged me to give it a try. I did. I made it to the finish line and was so proud of myself! I could also see how proud my children were of me. My daughter is very quiet, but loves acting. I think she, with a little more encouragement from me, will try out for the next school play. I guess being a role model is important!"

Kids bear witness to the power of healthy self-esteem. Seven-year-old Jake told me, "My mom knows everything. She tells me I can be anything I want when I grow up. I want to be a scientist and look at bugs under a microscope. I know I am smart just like my mom." Jake and his mom both have healthy self-esteem. Their confidence shows up in these few sentences.

Liz, age thirteen, says, "Now that my mom is in recovery, we have a better relationship. We do more together. I know I am important to her. Even when we are in a disagreement, we don't yell or curse one another anymore. We have agreed to wait until we can talk respectfully to one another. I feel so much better about myself. And about her too. It's also helping me communicate better with my dad and my friends."

JOURNALING ACTIVITY

1. Write about something you've done that made you proud.

2. What do you remember about your mother's self-esteem? How was yours as a child?

3. Write about a time when you knew your "Wise Woman" (that intuitive voice) was encouraging you.

4. Describe your Gremlin. Draw it if you like. What does it look like? Is it male or female? What does it say to you? How do you silence your Gremlin?

5. Make a list of at least five ways that you can be kind to yourself. Put them up on the refrigerator or your mirror to remind you.

6. How do you want your self-esteem to look and feel one year from now?

7. What do you need to do in order to accomplish that?

8. Make a list of what you do well and enjoy doing.

9. Make a list of your children's strengths. Share it with them and see if they have anything to add or delete.

10. Create a system so that each of your children has a few age-appropriate chores.

GEMS FOR YOUR POCKET

Give your children genuine praise, but do not overpraise.

Give your children lots of encouragement.

Resist comparing your child to siblings or anyone else.
No one likes to be compared.

Be a positive role model.

Be present with your child regularly.

Talk some. Listen more.

Treat yourself and those around you with respect.

Catch your child being good. Acknowledge the positive behavior.

At the end of every day, your child needs and deserves to hear
two things: "I love you," and "Tomorrow's a new day."

Allow your children to participate in the extracurricular activities they enjoy.

"Believe in your dreams and they may come true. Believe in yourself and they will come true." (Anonymous)

AFFIRMATIONS

I am confident.

I respect myself, my children, and others.

I treat myself with kindness and understanding.

I surround myself with positive and encouraging people.

I am a strong and determined woman.

I am creating the life I desire and deserve.

I am proud of myself.

I am a positive role model.

I am strong in my recovery.

I am enough.

CHAPTER 7

Discovering your priorities

One hundred years from now it will not matter what kind of car you drove, what kind of house you lived in, how much you had in the bank account or what your clothes looked like. But the world may be a little better because you were important in the life of a child.

—*Margaret Fishback Powers*

You are working hard to build the life that you dream of. I imagine the dream consists of remaining in your recovery, raising happy and healthy children, being a responsible citizen, having shelter and a steady job, and more. You are now able to take care of yourself and your children. Having a strong community and fellowship that supports you is also important.

Every mom wants to succeed. Every mom wants to have the things that are most important to her for herself and her family. Looking at the many skills and tasks you've already achieved shows your success. This chapter will help you clarify what is most important to you in your life. We'll also look at the parts that can sometimes take extra time and energy, yet are not serving you. Sometimes, they can creep into your life without you even realizing it.

Paloma said, "As long as I have a loving relationship with my children, my recovery, and my health, my life is full. I don't know what I would do without these treasures in my life. While a new car and a house would be really nice, I am okay without them."

Andrea added, "I want my kids to get a good education. I want them always to know that I love and support them. Education is important to me. They can do anything they want with their lives. A good education can help."

Children want to know that they are safe and secure. They want to have a mom who protects them. A mom who provides shelter, food, clothes, and other necessities. A mom who is there for them, even when they are having a bad day. A mom who loves them, no matter what.

Connor said, "I want my mom to quit talking *at* me. I want her to listen to me. When she does, I feel loved. I usually get into a better mood. What I really want is for my mom to stay in her recovery. My life is so much better now than it was when she was using drugs. She is very different from how she used to be. I also want my brother to get help. He is only twenty-two, but he is an addict just like my mom. I worry about him a lot. I'm afraid he will end up in prison or die. He and my mom are my only family. I don't know what I would do without them."

Lisa, age fifteen, said, "I want my mom to be home when I come home at night. I want her to be interested in what I am doing and who my friends are. I don't want her to try and be my best friend. I want her to be my mom. I like it when she is interested in what I'm doing. Most Saturdays, she goes to my soccer games. I don't talk to her, but I am proud that she is there. It makes me feel loved and important."

Looking Back so you can Move Forward

Many of you grew up with parents who had different priorities than you do. If you came from a home where there were drugs and alcohol, your parents' priorities were possibly doing whatever they had to do to get their drugs. You were not seen as a child during these times. You were not parented in the way that you needed or deserved. The old saying, "Children should be seen and not heard" applied to many of you. Today, the saying goes, *Children should be seen and should be heard.*

If you came from a home that did not have drugs and alcohol, you may have been raised by parents who made sure there was food on the table, a roof over your head, and shoes on your feet, but who didn't necessarily see their job as parents to include raising children with high self-esteem and good communication skills.

Regardless of how you were raised, most of you have made the conscious choice to do it differently today. You can. With support and some new tools in your parenting toolbox, you can give your children a different experience growing up than you had.

Juanita said, "I lived with both parents. They worked very hard and were always tired. They were doing all that they could to make enough money so we could live in a house. We always had plenty to eat. My dad felt that providing for his family was the most important thing he could do. When my mom wasn't at work, she cooked and cleaned a lot. This was how she showed her love to her family. My parents always made sure that one of them took us to Mass every week. Religion was also very important to both of them."

Ruth added, "Drinking and partying were all my parents cared about. They let me do whatever I wanted as long as I didn't ask them for money or anything. I learned to stay away as much as I could. Otherwise, I just hid out in my room. I hated it. I wanted their attention, but we always ended up in a fight because they were drunk. Now that I am in recovery, I realize how much we all missed when we were children. They don't even know us. I am so grateful to be parenting my children differently. I want to have a strong and loving relationship with my children always."

GOLF BaLLS, PebbLes, and sand

I strolled into my philosophy class one day to find two empty jars sitting on the desk, along with some golf balls, some pebbles, and some sand. I couldn't imagine what we were going to do with them. On the board, the instructor wrote: "Your life in a jar." Curiosity rose in the room. Without a word, she filled one jar with golf balls.

She asked, "Is the jar full?"

It looked full to most of the class. She then poured in the pebbles. We watched as they filled in the spaces between the golf balls.

She asked, "Now is the jar full?"

Heads nodded. Now the jar was full. She then poured nearly two cups of sand into the jar. The sand filled in every possible crevice.

"Now is the jar full?" she asked.

"Yes," the class agreed. "The jar is full." But we still didn't know what she was actually doing.

Holding up the jar now full of golf balls, pebbles, and sand, she began to explain. "This is your life. The golf balls represent the most important parts of your life. Even if you lost everything else, as long as you had them, you would be okay. The pebbles are the second most important things in your life. You may want and need them, but they are not quite as critical as your golf balls. You would be okay even if you lost them. They could be replaced. The sand is everything else that fills up your life. It takes up space, but adds little or no benefit."

She then filled an empty jar with sand.

"What does this jar tell you?"

One brave soul said, "If we fill our lives up with sand, there isn't any room for the important things in our lives." As she nodded that his response was correct, she handed each of us a piece of paper. The paper had three columns: Golf Balls, Pebbles, Sand. The instruction read: Make a list of what you consider to be in each of the categories, which were defined as follows:

Golf balls: Most important in your life. Even if you lost everything else, you would be okay (i.e., children, sobriety).

Pebbles: Important in your life, but less so than golf balls. You could do without if you had to (i.e., job, car).

Sand: All of the other stuff that fills your life. It adds very little or nothing positive (i.e., drama, TV, gossip).

Before you read any further, take a few minutes and make your own three lists. You can add more as you think of them.

GOLF BALLS	PEBBLES	SAND

What is most important to you? What do you want out of life? What do you want your life to look like next year? What about five years from now? Once you answer these questions, you can make conscious choices as you create the life you want and deserve. If you don't yet know what is really important to you, your jar may fill up with pebbles and sand rather than golf balls.

Here's a list of priorities that some moms came up with in a parenting class:

GOLF BALLS

Recovery · My children · Family · Fellowship · Myself
Health · Spirituality · Sponsor · Music · Nature · Job · Money

PEBBLES

Medicine · Car · Shelter · Money · Clothes · Job
Clothes · Fellowship · Support group · Exercise · Sponsor
Healthy friendships · Driver's license · Furniture · Books · Pets

SAND

Jewelry/piercings · Resentment · Anger · Money · Vacations
Hair care · Bad language · Men · Makeup · Negative attitudes
Drama · Chaos · Ego · Drugs · Self-pity · Pets · TV · Alcohol
Guilt · Worry · Friends that are not a good influence
Toys · Depression · Stripping · Nail polish · Music · Coffee

As you can see, many of the categories are specific to one area. Others appear in more than one list. To some, a job and money may be a golf ball. To others, while they would like to have them, they know they would be okay without them. They can find a new job and make more money if necessary. And isn't it interesting how much longer the sand list is than the golf ball list?

As a mom, you have many responsibilities. It's important to be very clear on what is most important to you. You only have so much time and energy in your twenty-four-hour day. If you are not clear on what your golf balls are, you may end up giving your time and energy to people, places, and events that are not really a priority.

Diana said, "Last year, I volunteered to be in charge of my son's school fund-raiser. It was more work than I anticipated. While I wanted to support his school, it was hard, because my kids found themselves home alone a lot for nearly three months while I was at the school organizing. The school made money, but my kids lost out on having me around after school and in the evenings. Their behavior changed. There was more fighting and bickering. They missed me. I learned my lesson. I will find some other way to help the school that doesn't take me away from my children and our family time."

Liz added, "I started working extra hours because my boss was shorthanded. By the time I got home, the kids hadn't done their homework. Dinner was nowhere to be seen. The house was a mess. I was exhausted. We were all yelling before I even got my jacket off. I realized that I need to leave work on time. It's a challenging time of day. It goes much better if I am there. My kids need me. Giving extra time to help out my boss was important, but my family is more important."

Ann said, "Where I live, there is way too much sand. Every time I walk outside, there are moms sitting around talking. That would be fine, except that everything they are talking about is sand.

Gossip and drama. I don't join them anymore. I don't want any extra sand in my jar."

When you are clear about your priorities, there's more meaning in your life. Even with the many demands of being a mom and your busy schedule, life will be less rushed and chaotic. At the end of the day, you will most likely feel better about yourself, because you have given your time and energy to what and who is most important in your life.

As you take care of your golf balls, you may discover that other parts of your life also work better. For example, your health is a golf ball. If you are doing what you need to do to take care of your health, you will feel better physically and mentally. When you feel better, you are better equipped to care for yourself and your children.

Your recovery is definitely a golf ball. It deserves the very best care possible. It takes time and energy. You know what you need to do in order to maintain your recovery. It may be going to meetings, seeing your sponsor, reading, praying, exercising, or all of the above. It not only needs, it deserves, your time and energy.

Every single mom I've ever done this process with considers her children to be a golf ball. I remember the first time I heard a mom of four children say, "It's a privilege, not a right, to be a mom." At one point in her life, she had had her children removed from her because of her addiction. Going into recovery and eventually getting her children back changed her view of being a mom. What a wise mom she is! Your children are miraculous gifts that you have been given. It is your responsibility to be their protector, their loving guide, their teacher. They depend on you to help them grow up to become independent, loving, responsible people one day.

sorting the golf balls from the sand

Find ways to honor, protect, and nurture the golf balls in your life. One way I do this is to share my list frequently with a friend. It helps me keep my priorities in order. Sometimes, I see that I have more sand than I realized. I begin that very day releasing the sand. When I have too much sand, there is not enough room for my golf balls. Occasionally, important parts of my life are not working as well as I'd like. Once I do this little exercise, I realize it's because I am not giving those areas my time and energy. I am too stuck in the sand. As soon as I rid myself of the chaos and drama, I am more attentive to what's really important, and life gets better once again.

Many times, your mind spins in thought about someone or a situation. Decide if it is a golf ball, a pebble, or just sand. You will know which category it fits into. If it's sand, take the steps to release it. Pray. Write. Speak. Do whatever will help you to let go. Sometimes, I simply pray, "Help me to let go of everyone and everything that is not part of my divine path."

When you know that something is a pebble or sand, make a plan to find a solution or resolution. Be proactive. Often, there is something you can do that will move you forward. Sometimes, being proactive is being silent. Be silent in prayer, rather than letting your thoughts spin. Pray that you can let go of what is taking your mind away from what is most important.

If you keep your jar full of sand, you don't have to focus on what really matters to you. Sand can give you permission not to hold your recovery, yourself, and your children as the most important areas of your life. It can convince you that you don't have to look at your past, that you can abandon your twelve-step work, or that you don't have to be honest or responsible. With sand, all you really have to do is keep your life full of meaningless things and events. You can keep people in your life who do not hold you accountable, or support you in your recovery, or encourage you to be all that you can be. You can ignore the wounds that are calling to be healed if you cover them up with sand.

A young woman, Margo, said, "I used to try to help everyone else solve their problems. I liked feeling important. I liked the drama and chaos. Through my own twelve-step work, I realized that this was one of the ways that I was keeping myself from looking at my own life, past and present. It was much easier to look at someone else's life rather than the mess I had made of my own."

Once Margo saw what she was doing, she had choices to make. She could keep filling her life with sand. Or she could let go of the sand and begin healing her own life. Margo was wise. She chose that her first step would be to learn ways to let go of the sand in her life.

She began with prayer. "Help me to see when I am putting sand in my jar. Gently remind me to let go of unnecessary chaos and drama." Then she asked a friend to please hold her accountable for what she was putting in her jar. The second sentence of the Serenity Prayer rang true for her—she needed "the courage to change the things I can."

Margo also chose not to be around certain people who spent most of their time gossiping and bad-mouthing others. She soon noticed that she did not even miss hanging out with them. Her days were more productive and enjoyable. She felt better about herself. When she did notice that she had gotten too involved in someone else's chaos, she was gentle with herself. She was changing a pattern that had been hers for a long time. Sometimes, she wrote in her journal as another way of letting go.

More than once, I have thought, "Hooray for me! I finally took another street!" But before I knew it, I was saying "Oops. Here I am back where I started." Here's another piece of Refrigerator Wisdom by Portia Nelson that has helped me at times like these.

Autobiography in Five Short Chapters*
by Portia Nelson

Chapter One
I walk down the street.
There is a deep hole in the sidewalk.
I fall in.
I am lost.... I am helpless.
It isn't my fault.
It takes forever to find a way out.

Chapter Two
I walk down the same street.
There is a deep hole in the sidewalk.
I pretend I don't see it.
I fall in again.
I can't believe I am in this same place.
But, it isn't my fault.
It still takes a long time to get out.

Chapter Three
I walk down the same street.
There is a deep hole in the sidewalk.
I *see* it is there.
I still fall in ... it's a habit ... but,
my eyes are open.
I know where I am.
It is *my* fault.
I get out immediately.

Chapter Four
I walk down the same street.
There is a deep hole in the sidewalk.
I walk around it.

Chapter Five
I walk down another street.

Many times, when I thought I had found a new way, I have found myself back in chapter 2, or chapter 3, or chapter 4. You just have to keep looking for that other street that will take you where you want to go. I ran into Margo almost a year after our first conversation. She shared how interesting it was to her that, once she made the shift away from drama and chaos—the sand in her jar—her life got better. She began working on herself and her relationship with her own mom and her two children. "It's work. I feel so much better about myself. I know what's really important to me. I'm not sure why, but people don't bring their drama and chaos to me as much anymore. When I do find myself getting sucked in or even inviting drama, I think of Portia Nelson's poem. I choose another street. It gets a little easier every time. I am so much happier."

As Margo made her shift, those around her shifted too. It's a dance. When you change your step, the people around you have no choice but to change theirs as well. Many times, the shift is unconscious, but it does occur. Imagine you are taking a walk with a friend. She decides to take the path to the right. You can choose to go that way and walk with her. Or you can choose to go to the left and walk by yourself. The bottom line is that her shift requires that you make a choice.

Audrey, mom of two teens said, "Once I started being consistent in my rules about the boys' curfew, they began coming home on time. Until then, I had threatened, but never followed through.

And so, our dance had been that I would threaten them with restrictions and they would stay out as late as they wanted because they knew I wouldn't follow through. Once I changed my step and followed through on what I said, they changed their step by coming home on time. It sure is a dance that just never stops; it just changes."

JOURNALING ACTIVITY

1. Look back at your lists of your golf balls, pebbles, and sand. Write why you chose the ones you did for each category. What do you gain or lose from each one?

2. Write how you are going to take care of each of your golf balls. For example: I keep my children safe. I provide them with their needs. I spend quality time with them regularly.

3. Write what you are going to do to take care of your pebbles. For example: I have a steady job. I am a good worker. I show up on time. I am reliable and trustworthy. I make enough money to care for me and my children.

4. Do you have too much sand in your jar? What do you know about it? What does it represent? Why do you keep the sand?

5. If you want to rid yourself of the sand, what steps are you going to take?

6. What do you want your life to look like twelve months from now? Five years from now? What do you need to do in order to accomplish these goals?

Dream big! You may be pleasantly surprised!

We all have golf balls in our lives. These are the things that are most important to us. If you lose everything else, you will still be okay as long as you have these. For example: your sobriety, your children, and your health. Protect, honor, respect, and nurture your golf balls. Give them your best.

While your pebbles are important, you can still have a good life even if you lose them. For example: Even if you lose your job, you can always get another one.

Sand represents the unnecessary stuff that takes up more of your time and energy than is good for you. For example: gossip, drama, negative attitudes.

Give your time and energy to your golf balls first and foremost.

Let go of your sand.

Do whatever helps you to let go. Pray, write, walk, talk with a friend.

Share your three columns with a friend now and then. It will help you keep what's most important to you in the forefront.

AFFIRMATIONS

I am clear on my priorities.

I hold my golf balls deep within my heart.

I give them the time and nurturance that they deserve.

I let go of the sand.

I am free of gossip, drama, and negative attitudes.

My higher power helps me to let go.

I spend my time wisely.

I release everyone and everything that is not part of my divine plan.

I am strong.

I am enough.

CHAPTER 8

Gratitude and Acknowledgment

If the only prayer you say in your whole life is
"Thank you," that would suffice.

—*Meister Eckhart*

Every mom wants to feel appreciated, to be acknowledged for her hard work, for all she does as a mom. Every mom wants to know that she is important in her children's lives. I am frequently asked: "When will my kids appreciate all that I do for them? Why aren't they grateful for anything?" My response is not always what they want to hear. For me, the real gratitude and acknowledgment came sometime around when my children were in their second year of college. They began phoning, usually for one of three reasons: "Please send money or a care package of chocolate-chip cookies," or "Mom, I am so sorry for all of the headaches and worries I caused you," or "Mom, Thank you for all you did for me all those years. It's not so easy being on my own. I really do appreciate and love you."

Being a mom is no easy venture. *Other than your recovery, being a mom is the most important and the most challenging thing you will ever do in your life.*

Children also want to be appreciated and acknowledged. You may think that they have it easy. All they have to do is go to school, do their homework and chores, and get along with you and their siblings. Those tasks alone are not necessarily easy for any child. Children want to be seen and understood by you, as well as by the other important people in their lives. They want to please you and get your approval.

Looking Back so You can Move Forward

I have heard very few moms say that they were shown appreciation as children. When they were acknowledged, it was usually because their parents were criticizing or punishing them.

Ann said, "The only time I remember any kind of an acknowledgment was when I kept my brothers out of the way and quiet while my parents partied."

Jen added, "I lied to the police in order to protect my dad one time. When he shut the door, he did mumble something about being glad that I covered for him. I was so torn. I didn't want to get him arrested, but I also felt so guilty lying to the police."

Maddie offered, "My mom was never satisfied. When I was ten, I got my two younger siblings ready for school, gave them breakfast, and got them on the bus every morning. When I got home from school, if my mom said anything at all, it was that I had left a mess in the kitchen. These were the kind of acknowledgments that I knew about. They weren't anything that I looked forward to."

Because of these past experiences, expressing gratitude may be a new concept for most of you. But expressing gratitude is very important. When you chose recovery, you began a new way of life—a life that has much goodness to offer you. Believe it or not, the universe is full of abundance. *True abundance begins when you express gratitude and thankfulness.*

When you acknowledge what you do have at this moment in your life and what you are grateful for, more goodwill come to you.

In order to attract more of the things you desire, you must genuinely appreciate what you already have.

There's that old question: "Is the cup half empty or half full?" Look at the parts of your life that are at least half full. Express thankfulness for them. Nurture and care for the good things in your life. Appreciate them. They will grow.

For example, you live in a very small space. It is, however, safe and secure. Instead of spending words and energy complaining that it is too small, give thanks that you and your children are safe and secure—that you are together.

Many moms spend time regretting the past. You may regret how you parented your children before recovery. I encourage you to let that go. Be grateful for your children. You are doing what you need to do to rebuild and/or heal your relationship with them. Every day, express your gratitude for new chances and new opportunities, for continued strength and determination, that your heart and mind are learning new ways to be the mom you want to be.

The past is the past. It does no good to dwell on those days. They are over. That was then. This is now. You are blessed to be living on this day. You can choose how to spend it. I encourage you to let go of any and all shame and regret. Move forward today with gratitude in your heart.

The Power of Gratitude

The more you express your gratitude, the more you'll have reason to express it.

Whether you call it your higher power, God, or the universe, there is a force that wants you to have a life of abundance. Believe it or not, a life far better than you have imagined awaits you.

Get into the habit of expressing statements of thankfulness every day. This can be a prayer, a simple thought, or a kind word. Integrate them into your being. Wait and see what happens.

Pema Chödrön once wrote, "Beginning to tune into even the minutest feelings of gratitude softens us . . . . If we begin to acknowledge these moments and cherish them . . . then no matter how fleeting and tiny this good heart may seem, it will gradually, at its own speed, expand" (from "Everybody Loves Something," *Shambhala Sun*, March 1998).

Melody Beattie, author of *Codependent No More*, agrees: "Gratitude unlocks the fullness of life. It turns what we have into enough, and more. It turns denial into acceptance, chaos into order, confusion to clarity. It can turn a meal into a feast, a house into a home, a stranger into a friend. *Gratitude makes sense of our past, brings peace for today, and creates a vision for tomorrow.*"

The Power of Acknowledgment

Acknowledgments are truthful, heartfelt observations that we share with other people. They help your child or anyone who receives them see and pay attention to a part of themselves that they may be missing.

You can also give yourself an acknowledgment. For example: "I acknowledge myself for reading to my child every day," or "I acknowledge myself for remaining strong in my recovery." I end each of my parenting classes with time for "acknowledgments and gratitudes." When I first began what I thought would be a simple ritual, I immediately discovered that, for the majority of moms, it was not simple. That first day, some giggled. Some swore. They were uncomfortable. Resistance was high. They had a hard time thinking of anything to say. Some just plain refused to do such a "weird and ridiculous thing."

Once again, these moms became my teachers. They quickly helped me understand that this was something that was foreign to them. Many had not ever been acknowledged by anyone in this way. It was embarrassing to say something good about themselves or about anyone else out loud. Once they had done it a couple of times, however, it became an important part of their day. Many even say that it is their favorite part of the day!

We started off by each person giving another mom in the circle an acknowledgment. For example:

"I acknowledge you for being more patient with your children this week."

"I acknowledge you for following through and going to two meetings this week."

"I acknowledge you for listening to me when I'm frustrated or upset. You are a good friend."

Once these women overcame the hurdle of having someone say something kind to them, they loved the acknowledgments! They shared that they always felt better. They felt more positive about themselves, their children, and their recovery when they were acknowledged. It was obvious how their energy went up when someone acknowledged them. Some examples:

"I am not usually proud of myself until someone reminds me that I am doing something right. It makes me want to keep doing all that I can in my recovery. Barbara would say it's called 'encouragement.'"

"Sometimes it feels awkward and that's why I giggle, but I do like to hear nice things about myself. I am working hard. It feels good that others can see it."

For the majority, this may have been their first experience at receiving positive feedback ever. There were usually tears, hugs, and laughter that went along with this simple ritual.

Next, I asked the group to give themselves an acknowledgment. This was also new. While I could see many areas that they could acknowledge about themselves, it was not always so obvious to them. I asked them to dig as deep as they could—to find that one thing that they are proud of about themselves. The room quieted. The pride entered.

"I acknowledge myself for getting honest with myself and my counselor this week. It feels good."

"I acknowledge myself for taking responsibility for my past actions."

"I acknowledge myself for showing up for class today."

Their smiles and tears were genuine and touching. The good feelings spread around the room.

The guidelines for this ritual are simple:

1. Be genuine in your acknowledgment.

2. Look into people's eyes as you acknowledge them.

3. If you are receiving the acknowledgment, look into the giver's eyes.

4. Open your heart and your mind to give and receive the words.

But even though the guidelines are simple, this is no easy undertaking. Once again, after a few times of feeling somewhat uncomfortable, it is obvious how much both the giver and receiver enjoy the exchange. They are both benefiting.

You can begin giving daily acknowledgments to yourself, to your children, and to other important people in your life. You don't need to be in a group; this can happen anywhere.

For example, to your children: "I really appreciate you mowing the lawn without being asked. You are becoming very responsible," or "Jen, I want to acknowledge you for really listening to what your dad had to say before jumping in. You are changing your ways of communicating with him."

The benefits of acknowledgment are the same for your children as they are for you:

1. Acknowledgments feel good to give and receive. When you hear something positive about yourself, you tend to want to repeat that behavior. One mom told me, "When I thank my son for helping me carry in the groceries, he smiles. The next time I drive in and begin unloading the car, here he comes."

2. Acknowledgment can increase cooperation. Another mom: "When my kids are cooperative while we run errands, I simply acknowledge them for getting along and for their patience. Running errands is not their favorite thing to do. But they do feel good that I noticed their behavior."

3. Acknowledgment builds healthy self-esteem, as in "I acknowledge you for getting up on your own every day this week. That shows how responsible you are."

sharing Gratitude and Acknowledgment

There are many ways to integrate gratitude and acknowledgment into your daily life. Here are a few simple examples.

MEALTIME

Create a tradition of having a regular meal together. Turn off the TV, the music, cell phone, computer, or anything that will be distracting. This is the time for you to be together and connect as a family. Before you begin eating, go around the table and share one thing you are grateful for. With young children, it doesn't much matter what they say. What matters is that they become accustomed to giving and receiving gratitude.

When I first started this with my three children, I sometimes wondered, "Why, oh why did I think this was a good idea?" Here's an example of a typical time. The four-year-old was thankful for her cat (she didn't have a cat). The eleven-year-old was thankful that we weren't having meatloaf. The thirteen-year-old was thankful that he only had two sisters. Sound familiar? I took some quiet deep breaths and moved on with dinner. It was not a time to judge, advise, lecture, or criticize. The good news is that, over a period of time, they did get more comfortable with naming something that they were grateful for. Interestingly enough, now that they have young children of their own, guess what they do at dinnertime? Yep. The very same ritual. In spite of their resistance, they did benefit from it.

GRATITUDE JOURNALS

Many years ago, Oprah started something called gratitude journals. She recommended that you get a notebook just for expressing gratitude. Every day, you start the day by writing at least five things that you are grateful for. The five soon grow to fifteen. The fifteen soon grow to twenty-five. And on and on. Once you start listing everything you are grateful for, you just keep thinking of things and wanting to get them all on your list. They may include things as simple as an ice cream cone, or things as vital as your recovery. And everything in between. There's no right or wrong. After doing this a few times, your energy increases. You develop a more positive outlook on your life. Keep writing. It's fun.

FAMILY GRATITUDE JOURNALS

Some families get a notebook and leave it somewhere, like in the kitchen, where anyone can jot gratitudes down whenever they feel like it. It's fun to see how many things you come up with as a family. It also can be a great way to have a nice conversation during or after a meal. Take a little time and talk about all of the things that are in your family journal. I call them "gratefuls." Your family may use the same word or something different.

As the mom, take the lead. Get the journal. Ask one of your kids if he or she wants to decorate the cover. Begin putting in "gratefuls" regularly. They will come around. If you decide to do something like this, I recommend that, when the notebook is filled, you date it and tuck it away for when your children are older. You will all appreciate looking back at it down the road.

POCKET JOURNALING

Every mom in my class receives a little spiral notebook. They put the word "Gratitudes" and their names on the front. Then we start a timed process. They open to the first page and write one thing about themselves that they are grateful for. When I say "Pass," they pass their journals to the person on their left and write one acknowledgment about that person in the journal that has come to them from the person on their right. When I say "Pass" again, they continue the process until they have written an acknowledgment in each person's journal. Each person ends up with acknowledgments from all of the other moms in the class.

Once their journals come back to them, the room always quiets as they read what others have written about them. Some choose to share their favorite acknowledgments. Others want to keep them just for themselves. I encourage them to add more acknowledgments to their own journals anytime they want and to open them throughout their week, whenever they need a little extra goodness coming their way. This can give important inspiration and encouragement.

This is something that you can do with your children as well. If they are too young, you can write the entries for them. Every month or so, pull the journal out and go through the process again. Over a period of time, you will all end up with a meaningful journal of gratitudes. This can also become a wonderful holiday tradition. Everyone can bring a simple little journal, and you can all play the "pass the journal" game described above. It's very fun and fills your heart all at the same time.

A HOLIDAY TRADITION

When I was beginning to establish traditions in my own home, I bought a plain white tablecloth and some indelible colored felt-tip pens. (The pens may say permanent marker. Any kind of pen that won't wash out will work.) Thanksgiving was at my house that year. The tablecloth was on the table and I had placed little cups of pens here and there. After the dishes were cleared from dinner, I asked that everyone write or draw something on the tablecloth that they were thankful for. They could do it anytime during the day. It became quite an activity. The creative people were right there and eager to create their piece. The less creative were stewing and procrastinating about what they could do. By the end of the day, everyone, from the youngest baby to the eighty-eight-year-old great-grandmother, was represented on the table-cloth. People enjoyed reading what others had drawn or written. For the babies, we drew their little handprints or footprints and noted their date of birth.

The tablecloth was washed and put up until the following Thanksgiving, when it found its way to the table again. It usually takes about five years for us to fill up a tablecloth. And then we start a new one. Every so often, I pull them all out on Thanksgiving and everyone enjoys remembering their past gratitudes. It became a tradition and still is today. It's a wonderful way to celebrate new babies coming into our family and to remember those who have passed on during the year.

Some moms have begun their own tablecloth tradition for each of their children's birthdays. My sister does hers on New Years Day. It is such a simple thing and yet brings family, friends, and children all together in a unique and lasting way. If you decide to start something like this, please remember that this is meant to be a fun activity. If the young children just want to draw lines or circles and scribble, let it be. It is not about the quality of their creativity, but rather about a wonderful way to bring joy and laughter into the day. And, most likely, you will be creating a new tradition for your family.

scott's shoebox

Everyone needs encouragement. Sometimes we need more than others. When my kids were in grammar school, occasionally I'd draw a happy face on their napkins as I packed their lunches. When they opened them at school, they smiled and knew I was thinking of them. As they got older, if they were struggling with a friend or going to have a test, I'd write little notes to remind them that I was thinking of them as they went through their school day. I wasn't doing it with a lot of consciousness. I think it was just kind of fun. I don't recall that they ever even commented about my little "love notes."

As my son went through his teen years, he became a pretty angry young man. Our communication became more and more difficult. It was during these times that I often found myself writing to him, because our verbal communication was not working. I left little notes under his pillow, or sometimes on his windshield—notes of encouragement that life would get better for him, that he was loved. He never said a word about any of them. At the time, a part of me worried that even this attempt was not reaching him. I just kept writing.

Many years later, he and his wife had their first baby. I was there to help them through the first few days. I don't recall how the conversation came up, but all of a sudden, he said, "Just a minute, Mom" and disappeared into their guest room. A couple of minutes later, he returned with a shoebox in his hands, a shoebox that was decorated in wallpaper that I immediately recognized from his childhood days.

He sat down, not saying a word, and opened the box. There was every single lil' love note I had ever written him. Napkins with happy faces from second grade to "Hang in there" notes that I had left for my angry teenage son. Tears streamed down our faces. "Mom," he said, "There were so many times I felt like such a loser.

I couldn't do anything right. You have no idea how many times I would sit on my bed and read through these notes. Many times, it's what kept me going. Thank you."

I share this story with you as an example of the power of a simple happy face or a few words. Sometimes we need to write acknowledgments. It allows the other person to read them privately in his or her own time.

Continue to trust your intuition as a mom. If something tells you to draw a happy face on a napkin, do it. Have no expectation of a "Thank you." The thank you will show up in some other way.

There were times when I would have appreciated an acknowledgment from Scott, but I realized that I was doing this for him, not for me. When you truly give a gift, there are no strings attached. You receive the joy in giving the gift. How or when the person chooses to receive the gift is not up to you. As a mom who was worried about her son, this helped me to feel as if I were doing something that might support him. And that was a gift to me.

Words of acknowledgment and encouragement are powerful. They cost nothing.

They are always right there within you. Use them. You and your child will benefit in ways seen and unseen.

JOURNALING ACTIVITY

I.   Begin a list or journal of your gratitudes today.

2.   Write at least five gratitudes in it every day.

3.   Write at least five self-acknowledgments.

4.   Write and share an acknowledgment with each of your children and with others that are important to you.

5.   How do you feel when you give an acknowledgment?

6.   How do you feel when you receive an acknowledgment?

7.   Are there any gratitude traditions that you want to begin? If so, what are they?

GEMS FOR YOUR POCKET

The more you express your gratitude, the more you have reason to express it.

Other than your recovery, being a mom is most likely the most important thing you'll ever do in your life.

It may also be the hardest thing you'll do in your lifetime.

Your child wants and deserves acknowledgments from you.

Find ways to express your gratitudes every day.

Begin teaching your children to give and receive gratitudes.

Saying thank you is a gratitude.

An acknowledgment from you may help your children want to repeat the behavior that you just acknowledged them for. Catch them being good.

Even in hard times, there is always something to be grateful for. Look for it, it's there.

AFFIRMATIONS

I acknowledge myself daily.

I acknowledge my children daily.

I extend a genuine smile, a "thank you," a kind word to at least five people every day.

I deserve to have good in my life.

I move forward today with an open heart that is full of gratitude.

I am grateful for all that I am and all that I am not.

I am strong in my recovery.

I am enough.

CHAPTER 9

The Power of Play and Laughter

> Laughter is the key to survival during the special stresses of child-rearing. If you can see the delightful side of your assignment, you can also deal with the difficult.
>
> —*James Dobson*

Every mom would welcome days that include joy and laughter, days that lift her spirits. It is not uncommon to hear a mom say, "I don't have fun anymore. I wouldn't even know how. My old ways of having fun are no longer in my life. I'm in recovery, a mom of three, and I work full-time. When would I have time to have fun?"

You, like everyone else, simply feel better, more positive, when you have some laughter in your day. Recently, a mom said, "I work so hard. Why can't I just have something to laugh about once in a while?" The good news is she can. She may just need some help finding ways to lighten up and rediscover her humor.

According to life coach and *O* columnist Martha Beck, "The average adult laughs fifteen times a day; the average child, more than 400 times a day." We can all take a lesson from the children when it comes to play and laughter.

Every child wants to have days filled with lots of good play and laughter. They want a mom who sometimes participates in that fun and laughter. Laughing with them is quite different from laughing at them. No one wants to be laughed at. But it sure is fun when moms lighten up and share some humor and laughter with their children.

Can you imagine how wonderful it would be if, when your children are grown, they shared stories about how fun it used to be to laugh with you? How sometimes you were able to turn what could have been a moment of anger into humor?

Children not only want to play, they need to play. For young children, it is one of the most important ways that they learn. Wouldn't it be fun to learn through play? Actually, you do. When you play with your children, you can learn about a part of them that you may otherwise miss, as well as about a part of yourself that you may still be discovering.

Looking Back So You Can Move Forward

Kathy said, "The only time I remember either of my parents laughing is when they were partying or playing cards. It was never kid-appropriate humor. We heard it anyway. They laughed with the adults, but it was not ever acceptable for us to join in. Even though I didn't get the jokes, when I laughed, my dad yelled at me to shut up and get out of the room. I grew up associating laughter with drunken parents and dirty jokes."

Another added, "I was afraid to laugh out loud. When I did, I usually got hit for being rude. By a very young age, I had learned that laughing was not okay."

Kim offered, "What I most remember is that, when my sister and I started giggling about something, my parents, for a brief moment, thought it was funny and laughed too. When they laughed, we thought it was okay, and we laughed even more. Every time I looked at my sister, we laughed harder. Without any notice, one or both of my parents then got mad and told us to stop it—right now. It was not easy to stop. By the time they got really mad, the laughter was gone, and usually one or both of us was ready to cry. Usually, it was my dad who threatened us to knock it off and eat dinner. We finished in silence, feeling shamed. I remember thinking, 'How can we get in trouble for just laughing?'"

Johanna chimed in, "I don't remember my mom ever laughing. When we even giggled, she usually got mad and told us to be quiet. It was confusing. What were we doing wrong? I think she knew our laughter made my dad mad. She didn't want him to get angry. It was easier to try to make us be quiet than to deal with him. I suppose she was trying to protect us."

Caroline reflected, "I had an aunt who never had children. Maybe that's why she always let us laugh. She laughed with us. She always came with silly jokes or riddles to tell us. One time, she brought a magic act. We went crazy when she was there. My mom didn't say anything during these times. She gave us dirty looks and didn't participate. We didn't care, because we were having so much fun with Aunt Pat. But I knew my mom was mad at me."

we repeat what we see

We all learn from the significant adults in our lives about many things, including humor. Many of you, like the moms above, did not have a parental role model who delighted in humor and laughter. This may very well be one of the reasons you tend to be serious. Maybe you do not yet feel comfortable with play and laughter. You may have been raised to believe that, when you laugh, you are being immature, out of line.

Tracy said, "I don't ever recall my mom laughing, telling a funny story or joke, nothing. It's who she was. I didn't even realize that some moms actually have a sense of humor. When I got married, I came into a family where even the women share in the laughter. It is so much fun to be with all of them. I cannot even imagine what it would have been like to have had a mom who knew how to laugh and play."

Lisa shared, "I don't remember my mom ever showing any humor. I don't even recall her laughing. I don't think she did. I remember my dad laughing, but most of the time, it was from inappropriate jokes that us kids didn't get. I remember how awkward it felt when the adults were snickering and jabbing one another, but I didn't know why. It was embarrassing."

Do you remember a parent telling you to "Wipe that smile off your face"? How did that make you feel? Embarrassed? Shamed? Afraid? Before long, you learned that it was not okay to smile. Fear, anger, rejection, anxiety, and criticism can affect children at a very young age, causing them to grow up without a healthy sense of humor.

Gina shared, "I remember, more than once, being at the dinner table when my dad walked in from work. I immediately smiled, because I was so excited to see him. His response was, 'Kid, you wipe that smile off your face. There's nothing funny about me having to work twelve-hour days to put this food on the table and shoes on your feet. So, just knock it off.' Dinnertime became a dreaded event for all of us. We ate in silence most of the time. Unless we were getting a lecture or listening to my parents argue, there were no words during mealtime."

The only way to break this cycle is to learn new patterns of behavior. When I die, there will be a celebration of my life. I feel confident that all three of my children and others who know me well will all agree on one thing: "She had a great sense of humor. She loved to laugh." I imagine my oldest daughter will tell about the times that we got so silly I had to pull the car over until we could stop laughing. Sometimes, we didn't even know what we were laughing about. But once we started, we couldn't stop.

Do you know this kind of laughter? The kind that makes you think you're gonna pop or pee your pants? Don't you feel better when you have had a laugh like this?

As moms, we tend to get too serious. We forget that, sometimes, we actually communicate more effectively with our children if we lighten up and use some humor.

Many times, at the end of a long day, I could tell that one of my kids was on the edge, ready for a full-blown tantrum. These moments usually occurred at bedtime when I hadn't gotten them settled as early as I should have. I had the choice to "lay down the law" and experience the tantrum or, on a good evening, to choose to lighten up the situation by somehow lightening up myself.

Jackie added, "In my house, neither of my parents ever tried to help us get out of a bad mood. In fact, usually they said something or did something to antagonize me until I finally did throw a fit. Then they stood there and laughed at me. I always ended up crying. Once I started crying, my dad slapped me and pushed me into my bed. I cried myself to sleep many nights. Maybe they didn't know any other way. My mom used to say that that is exactly what her parents did to her when she was overtired and in a bad mood. That's why I am trying so hard to do it differently. It felt horrible when I was a kid."

Here's a story from my own experience. When my daughter was on the edge, overtired, and ready for a fight, I grabbed any old sock that was just lying around and put it on my hand. Good old Mr. Sock came to life. It worked every time. As the sock puppet started talking to her or being silly, she relaxed and calmed down enough to settle into her bed. It may sound silly. That's because it was silly. But try it sometime. The distraction of the sock and of me shifting my mood helped her to shift and settle for the night.

The mom of eleven-year-old Darcy heard me talk about Mr. Sock. One night, when she was desperate with Darcy, she found herself searching the floor for a sock. When she saw me a few days later, she said, "At first I felt so ridiculous, and Darcy said, 'how dorky, Mom.' But, it did do the trick. It dispelled the frustration between the two of us and the day ended on a good note."

A little humor goes a long way.

Learning Through Play

Young children learn through play. Many times, I've heard moms say, "My three- and four-year-olds go to preschool. All they do is play." True, it looks as if all they are doing is playing. That's their job. While it looks easy to us, it is not so easy to them. They are learning how to interact with other children and adults through play. They're developing communication and language skills, learning how to follow directions and be a part of a cooperative group. And they are learning age-appropriate problem-solving. Just as you may have a job that you go to many days a week, it is their job to learn these important skills.

When children play outside, make an art project, relax during story time, or share during snack time, they are learning. It is all part of how they learn the skills necessary for their development at this early age.

Studies show that play increases a child's development in many areas: intellectual, social, emotional, and physical. This is why it is so important for children to play every day. Physically active play—imaginative, creative, and artistic play—are all important for your young child to experience.

One mom said, "My daughter always wants to play the same thing every time I drop her off at school. I want her to do other things." Give her time. She will. There may be some skill that she is trying to develop—something she is trying to accomplish. You may or may not ever know what it is. She will, however, move herself on to something else when she is ready.

Children don't need toys to play. In fact, many children have too many toys. Toys that maybe they have outgrown. Toys that have missing pieces or broken parts. I encourage you to go through your child's toys about every three months. Get rid of the ones that are broken or have missing parts or are in other ways no longer usable. Pack them away or, better yet, pass them on to someone who can use them. If there still seem to be too many, box up half of them and organize the remaining half. It is easier for a child to find something to play with if there are fewer choices. When your child has lost interest in the toys you left out, unpack the ones you put away. Rotating their toys frequently is fun for them. They are excited to have some things that they haven't played with for a while.

Too many toys can be overwhelming and overstimulating for children. Think how it feels when you walk into a store and find pile after pile of whatever you're looking for. It's hard to focus, to find what you want. It's the same for your children. If there's a heap of toys in the corner of the room, you may notice that they seem to rummage through all of them, but really don't play with any of them. This is most likely because the toys are not age-appropriate or because there are simply too many of them. In the case of toys, less is more.

Liz has an almost-four-year-old son who loves his tools. She shared, "He loves to get them out, but then he won't pick them up." I asked her son to go get his toolbox and show them to me. He happily arrived back in the living room and proceeded to dump his toolbox onto the floor. There must have been somewhere between sixty and seventy pieces. As soon as they were dumped, he picked up a screwdriver, walked away from the heap of tools, and began playing with a truck and his one tool. Liz began getting frustrated, telling him to come clean up his mess, since he had dumped them all out. Of course, he just stared at the floor and went on playing with his screwdriver.

Sound familiar? I asked him to come and choose six of his favorite tools from the pile. We found a small box, and it became his toolbox. He was delighted, as was his mom. She quietly put the other pieces in a cupboard and said that she would rotate them every few days! Success! It was too overwhelming for him to play with all of the tools at once and cleaning them up was becoming a power struggle. When he appeared ready to move on, his mom handed him the box and calmly said, "Put your tools in your toolbox for next time." He did so without argument. He could handle putting away this many.

sand, dirt, and a bucket of water

When possible, encourage your children to play outside. Usually, some sand, dirt, and water will make for a far more enjoyable activity than many of the toys you are tempted to buy at the toy store. Children love to run, climb, and swing. Find places where you can enjoy the outdoors and nature together. It's amazing how a little bucket and shovel can keep a child entertained in a sandbox.

Bailey and I have "brown-bag adventures" or "bug hunts." She gets a brown lunch bag. We take a walk, and she enjoys putting twigs, leaves, rocks, anything she likes along the way in her bag. An adventure like this will typically last much longer than a bucket full of toys. Sometimes when we get home, she takes a piece of colored paper and a glue stick and makes a picture.

Here are some other ways moms have shared that they have created opportunities for quality play with their children.

DOWNTIME

Many children today say they just want some downtime—some time to just hang out, time when they don't have to be anywhere.

One afternoon while they were driving in the car, Maria's son, age six, said to her, "Mom, do you think maybe someday we could just stay home?" The mom chuckled. She then realized that he was serious. He was asking for some time when he didn't have to be running from activity to activity. She shared that, when she started being more aware of his need for downtime, they were all more relaxed. And when they do have to go somewhere, the kids seemed to complain less. Everybody needs time at home. Just to be. When we over-schedule ourselves and our children, there is little time for relaxation, for play, or for just being a family.

PLAYING AT WORK

Pam shared that she has found that there are many things that she does around the house that can actually become an activity for the kids. "It sometimes takes a little longer and more patience on my part, but if I involve them in my cooking, baking, gardening, or cleaning, they like to help for a while, and then it seems to help them to figure out something that they want to do. Recently, I had them help me weed a little flower bed. First thing I knew, they were digging and raking a little area, saying they wanted to get some seed to make their own garden. They spent the next two hours having fun in playing at their own project. My involving them initially helped them to get creative. It was a great afternoon."

A CREATIVITY BOX

A box of art supplies can many times help children turn a boring morning into a morning of fun activity. Put some crayons, paper, stickers, paint, clay, glue, or whatever is age-appropriate in it. Help set your children up in an area where they can be free to enjoy their creativity and not have to worry about spills. Cover your kitchen table or an outside table with butcher paper and see what they create on it. Children have wonderful imaginations. As the mom, you need to set the scene for them to create.

Please take note that I said "age-appropriate" supplies. Catherine, a mom of three, recently called me, sobbing into the phone. Her daughter, Cameron, almost five, had just cut her own bangs for the third time that year. She was very angry and had screamed at her, spanked her, and put her in her room. When Catherine composed herself a little, I asked, "Catherine, why did Cameron have the scissors?"

"I only went outside for a minute," she responded, "and when I came back, she had chopped her bangs all the way to the scalp. I am furious with her!"

"Since this is the third time that she has done this," I suggested, "maybe she's showing you that she isn't ready yet to have the scissors without supervision."

"Barbara, she's almost five," said Catherine. "She should be more responsible."

"Catherine, maybe she *should* be, but she clearly isn't just yet. She didn't do it to make you mad. She just wasn't thinking about her hair. She was simply enjoying the cutting. Give her a little more time. Take the scissors out of the box. When she wants to cut, you will know that you need to be right there. She'll get it one of these days."

Catherine began to cry again, and said, "I know you're right. I didn't think of it that way. She's so smart I sometimes forget that she's not yet even five years old."

Catherine went and got Cameron from her bedroom. After a hug, she told her that Mom would keep the scissors for her until she was a little older. Whenever she wanted to cut, she could just ask her mom for the scissors. Meanwhile, Cameron has plenty of supplies in her creativity box to make some beautiful pictures. The same strategy should apply to supplies like felt-tip pens, glue, or paint. Make sure that what you give your children in their creativity box is age-appropriate.

LIMIT SCREEN TIME

It is important to limit the amount of screen time your children have. They may plead and beg that all they want to do is watch TV. However, once the TV is turned off, they will find something to do that will be fun and more beneficial to them. When children spend too much time in front of the TV or computer screen, they miss out on play, whether it be riding their bikes, building a fort, or doing an art project. Age-appropriate play is far better than allowing your child to sit in front of the screen all day.

Many educators and pediatricians recommend no more than thirty to sixty minutes of TV a day. Half of that time should be spent with you watching with them and talking about what they can learn from the show. The television is not meant to be a babysitter. If you notice that you are using it this way, think about options that will be more beneficial for you and your children. And be sure you know what your children are watching. Remember, children—especially young children—absorb whatever they see and hear. While there are some worthwhile shows on TV, there are far more that are not appropriate or good for your child.

Moms Need Playtime Too

While it's important to learn to play with your children, it's also important for you to get to play without them sometimes. You may be wrinkling your forehead about now, thinking "What is she talking about?"

It's another form of self-care. You feel better when you have had a time to laugh and lighten up. *When you feel better, you are more patient and understanding with your children.*

We began a list of "playtime" activities for moms in one of my parenting classes. It may give you some ideas for yourself:

Baseball

Soccer

Watching a funny movie

Playing poker

Making a new recipe

Reading a funny book

See what else you can add to the list.

Have you ever spontaneously run through a sprinkler? Grabbed a ball and began shooting some hoops? Raced your child across the park? Just asking these questions in the class caused the group to start laughing, as they remembered some of the things that they have done to play.

Melanie said, "I recently went bungee jumping with my two teenagers. We had so much fun! Maybe more than the three of us ever had together. We laughed and screamed together. Ever since then, I notice that we are all getting along better. I think it was good for them to see their mom play."

Anita chimed in, "I took my kids to play miniature golf. I ended up playing too. We had so much fun together. They loved seeing me trying to get the ball in the hole. I enjoyed them and the day so much more than if I had just stood and waited for them to finish."

Sophia added, "We went camping with all four kids. We swam, played baseball. We even sang some corny songs. At the end of the day, the kids actually hugged me and said thank you for bringing them to such a fun place. They didn't realize that it was what we did together that really created the fun, not just the place. I felt so loved and grateful that night when I went to sleep. The playing helped me remember how good it feels to play."

Many moms say that their children always want them to play with them, but that it's hard—sometimes downright boring. "I don't know what to do with them," they say. "I have too many other things to do."

One mom related, "I wish my daughter had never gotten any Barbies. It's all she wants to do. If I have to play one more minute of Barbie, I am going to scream!" The group chuckled, because everyone knew exactly what she was talking about. It can be frustrating and boring to be playing with your child when you know you have many other things you should be doing or you are simply not enjoying the activity. For many moms, it is very hard to just get down on the floor and play with their children. As one mom recently said to me, "Barbara, I can only play Candyland so many times each day. That's all she wants to do with me."

One thing that can help is to sit down with your children and make a list of the things that you both enjoy doing. When you begin the Candyland game or the Barbie time, tell them that you are setting the timer for fifteen minutes. When the timer goes off, you can pick something from the list that everyone will enjoy.

Playing together helps you to feel closer to your children, and vice versa. You are most likely the most important person in your children's lives. Doing anything positive with you is important to them. Since play and laughter are so vital, they feel even better when you have shared some together. Make it a habit—part of your regular routine. Play is just another tool you can use to strengthen the bond you have with your child.

The Power of Humor

Using age-appropriate humor is an excellent parenting tool. Many times, due to factors like too much stress and being over-tired, moms get too serious. Some are afraid that, if they lighten up, their kids will take advantage of them. There are times when humor is not appropriate. However, there are many times when it can actually help both the mom and the child.

It's okay to lighten up. When you lighten up, your children may too. Remember, they are following your lead. In other words, if you are grumpy, they will most likely become grumpy. If you are feeling relaxed and calm, they will most likely be feeling the same way. *Model what you want to see.*

Jackson, age sixteen, shared this with me: "My mom used to yell constantly because us kids always left our wet bath towels on the floor. One day, I went in to take my shower and there's a little sign pinned to my towel, 'Please hang me up when you are done with me tonight.' I had to laugh. I imagined she chuckled when she walked in later that night and the towel was on the rack with a note, 'I'm just hangin' here. Thank you.'" This mom had found a way to get her son to hang up the towel using humor rather than yelling or nagging. The constant nagging was not only frustrating for mom, but also irritating for her son. The humor worked. You do not usually get a child's cooperation when you are yelling or nagging. Jackson not only hung up the towel; he returned a chuckle to his mom by leaving his own note.

Recently, in a parenting class, the group shared how they just wanted to laugh more. The following week, I handed each of them a small sealed envelope and asked them to sit quietly with their heads down. When they were ready, I told them, they should each open their envelopes and they would know what they needed to do. Meanwhile, they were to keep their heads down until I told them it was time to look up. We went through the process. When I said okay, everyone looked up. The room roared. Here was a room full of moms wearing big red clown noses. We could not stop laughing! We laughed and played with the red noses for a short time, and then we moved on with our day. The humor of this little process not only lightened everyone up as individuals, it brought them closer as a group. At the end of the day, many of them shared a gratitude about something that involved the laughter and the red noses.

Melody was the last one to share that day. With her voice faint and tears in her eyes, she said, "I felt like such a little girl this morning with my red nose. All day, I kept wishing that my mom had, just once, used humor. I get it. I get how different it can be for my kids. It's okay for me to be silly sometimes. Where do you get these red noses? I want to do it with my family."

Melody put words to what almost every mom in the room was feeling and thinking that day. After seeing me model the use of humor, they will be able to implement more of it with their children.

Laugh with 'Em, Not at 'Em

I've never seen anyone who didn't feel better after a good laugh, provided that others were laughing *with* them, not *at* them. Children, like everyone else, can be very sensitive. It is always important to make sure that they know you are laughing with them and not at them. Begin by noticing if your days go differently when your children get to laugh and be playful. What about the days when they want to laugh, but you are not in the mood for it? What about the days when you share some laughter?

Jasmine, age twelve, said, "When my mom breaks into a laugh, I can't help but laugh. The more I laugh, the more she laughs. Even if we have been arguing, we forget it. Our day gets better. It's like it cleans the air or something."

Thomas, age eleven, shared, "I worry a lot. Especially about taking tests at school. If my mom can make me laugh on the way to school, it helps. I start off feeling a little less anxious. My teacher tells me to think of something funny while she is passing out the tests. Sometimes, I am so nervous I start laughing and can't stop.

I end up getting in trouble. I don't feel better after that kind of laughter. I feel embarrassed."

Remember earlier I shared with you the story about my granddaughter being a flower girl? The night of the practice, she was halfway down the aisle and some well-meaning people chuckled because they thought she was so cute. She burst into instant tears. She thought they were laughing at her. Especially with young children, you need to make sure that they understand that you are laughing with them and not at them. No one likes to be laughed at.

Connie shared, "My dad was an alcoholic. The drunker he got, the funnier he thought he was. His humor was always inappropriate, usually having some kind of sexual connotation. He directed his comments at my sisters and me. We didn't like it. Many times, he was putting us down, and he just kept it up. When one of us either started to cry or yelled at him, he got worse. He didn't care about our feelings at all."

Margo shared, "I am way too serious, as are my children when they are around me. However, when they are with their friends or other family members, I notice how much more fun they are having. I know I'm the one who needs to learn to lighten up. As I do, they will. A friend told me to start out just watching a funny movie with them and laughing. That's what I'm gonna do. As a child, I don't remember any of the adults in my life ever laughing or being silly. It's no wonder I don't know how."

Melanie added, "My mom never laughed with me. She laughed a lot at me. I am trying very hard not to laugh at my children. Sometimes I do. I apologize and ask them to help me to laugh with them instead. I remember in eighth grade, my mom and I went to buy me a bathing suit. I came walking out in the one that I loved and she burst into laughter, telling me how ridiculous it looked. I was humiliated and ashamed. She tried later to apologize, but it didn't help at all. Every time I went swimming that summer, I felt self-conscious because of her reaction. Recently, my daughter and I went to buy her a bathing suit. From the dressing room, I heard her giggling. All of a sudden, she appeared in this hideous swimsuit, and we both burst out laughing. This was not laughing at her. It was laughing with her. The difference is she knew the silliness of the suit and had already had a chuckle about it. So she did not have to take our laughter personally."

Tiffany said, "My mom is such a dork sometimes. She tries to be funny, but it embarrasses me. So I ignore her, and then she gets mad. I think she tries to be the 'cool' mom. I don't want a 'cool' mom. I want a mom who acts like a mom rather than a kid."

Beth piped up, "My mom and I love to laugh together. We both try to make faces to make the other one laugh. Sometimes, even when I think she's going to get mad at me, she surprises me by using her silly voice and we both laugh."

Erin added, "I used to laugh at my mom's clothes or tease her about her hair. Once she quit putting me down, I eased up on her. Now we find other things to laugh about. When I was young, when I got mad, sometimes she looked at me and said, 'Turn that frown upside down 'cuz you're special.' As ridiculous as it was, I could never keep from laughing. To this day, it makes me laugh when she says it. I'll probably use it on my own kids."

Laughter is healing. But so are tears. Don't deny your tears. There will come a time, however, when they are no longer in your best interest—a time when you realize that you need to let go. Then you can begin to put what happened in the past into the past, and move forward to create your new life. Humor can help you move forward.

"Laughter is like changing a baby's diaper. It doesn't permanently solve any problems, but it makes things more acceptable for a while" (Author unknown).

JOURNALING ACTIVITY

1. How was humor handled in your home? Play and laughter?

2. Did your parents laugh with you or at you? How did that feel?

3. Make a list of ways you and your child can play together?

4. What might get in the way of playing with your child?

5. What are some of the ways for you to play?

6. Write about the last time you had a good laugh. Was it at anyone else's expense? How did you feel afterward?

GEMS FOR YOUR POCKET

Young children learn through play.

Lighten up when possible. A little humor can go a long way.

Organize and simplify your children's toys. Make sure they are safe and age-appropriate.

Recycle the toys if you have too many.

Include your child in some of your chores, like baking and gardening.

Turn off the TV. Enjoy the outdoors or create an art project.

Tears and laughter are both healing.

Children are sensitive. Make sure that you are laughing with them, not at them.

AFFIRMATIONS

I have at least five good belly laughs every day.

I laugh with my children, not at them.

I use appropriate humor.

I play on a regular basis with my child.

My child and I have a close relationship.

I find healthy ways for me to play regularly.

I am strong in my recovery.

I am enough.

CHAPTER 10

Taking care of yourself

The best thing a mother can give her child is a happy and fulfilled mom. There are many paths to happiness and fulfillment—follow your heart and choose your own way.

—*Lisa Hammond*

Every mom wants to feel good physically, mentally, spiritually, and emotionally. Being loving, kind, and patient to yourself and others is important.

There was a little oval wooden sign that hung in my great-grandmother's kitchen. "If mama ain't happy, ain't nobody happy." I remember reading it many times. I did not understand what it meant until I became a wife and mother.

You are the barometer for your family. If you are rested and feel good, the day tends to flow better for you and those around you. If you are having a "bad" day, others around you are affected. You are responsible for your own happiness. No one else can do it for you. Every mom wants to succeed. You want to be happy—to experience even the simple joys of life.

Every child wants to have good days. To most children, a good day is having fun, and getting along with their friends and their moms. They want a mom who doesn't take her bad moods out on them, a mom who takes good care of herself. When she does, she is a happier mom to be around.

Children want moms who are caring and patient. Moms who are willing to interact with them, listen to them, support them, believe in them. They may not know about the sign in my great-grandmother's kitchen, but they certainly know its message. They know that a "happy" mood makes for a much better day than a "bad" mood.

Joe, age nine said, "If my mom wakes up in a bad mood, before we even finish breakfast, there is already screaming and crying. I get into a bad mood. It takes me about two hours of being at school before I start to feel okay. I hate it when she's mad or upset about something else, but ends up screaming at us kids. We don't even have anything to do with it."

Every child wants to succeed. Part of succeeding is having a fun and a happy day.

Looking Back so you can Move Forward

Few of us had parents who took care of themselves in a healthy way. Many of our parents thought they were taking care of themselves and their families if they were working long hours, putting food on the table, and providing a roof over our heads. In part, they were.

Ginny said, "My mom thinks that moms today are too selfish. I like to go and exercise a few times each week, because then I am more patient with the kids. She tells me this is a waste of time. She was unhappy most of the time that I was growing up. She is still unhappy most of the time. It's no fun to be around her. It's amazing how one person who is in a bad mood can affect everyone else's moods. But she sure does. In spite of what she says,

I know that it benefits me, as a mom, when I find the time to exercise regularly."

Ann added, "My mom says that going to Mass every Sunday was how she took care of herself. She lived for that one hour each week. She says it was enough. It doesn't seem as if it was, because she was usually screaming and yelling at us during the rest of the week."

The good news is that many moms today know that they need to take better care of themselves, and want to do it. It's finding the time and knowing what to do that is the challenge.

Please remember that you are modeling good self-care for your children. Taking care of yourself shows them that you respect yourself and them enough to take the time to replenish yourself.

When my biological children were seven and nine, we adopted a baby girl from Korea. I had learned in the latter part of my first nine years of parenting the importance of taking care of myself on a regular basis. My third child grew up with a mom who knew how to take much better care of herself. As long as I saved a little of myself for myself, we were all much happier with how our days went. As adults now, my two oldest children have shared how much better life at home was once I started paying a little attention to myself. It was a gift, not only to me, but to them!

Learning to Love Yourself

The bottom line is, you need to love yourself. It is the foundation on which you can build to become the parent you genuinely want to be. It is nearly impossible to be a patient, understanding, and loving mom until you have learned to love yourself. As your love grows, you will become more accepting and confident of yourself. You will be strong in your awareness of who you are. You will not need to have your children or anyone else validate you. Self-love is your responsibility. It is an important piece of your continued inner work. As you keep learning to take care of you, the love within can grow.

You are worthwhile. You are a valuable and important person. You deserve to feel the very best you can, to have a healthy and happy life. Many moms discover that they give to everyone but themselves—their partners, their children, their parents, their neighbors, and others. *When you do not take care of yourself, you cannot be the mom, friend, or partner that you want to be.* When you take care of yourself, it benefits not only you, but the others in your life.

I asked a group of moms: "What gets in the way of your taking care of yourself?" They said:

No time.

No one to watch the kids.

I don't even know what I'd do.

I don't deserve anything good.

It costs money to do anything.

I feel guilty.

It won't help. Why try?

I'm too tired.

I'm lazy.

Do any of these sound familiar? I imagine they do. I also imagine that, on some level, you know that, when you do give yourself a little time to do something that makes you feel better, you are a happier mom. Usually, happier moms are more patient moms. Children with happier and more patient moms tend to be happier and more cooperative themselves.

Yellow flashing light! Warning! Self-care needed! Slow down!

Here are some signals that can help you realize that you are running on empty. Think of them as the warning light that goes on in your car when you are low on fuel. You car is telling you that it needs some attention very soon. You feel much better, more relaxed, when your tank is at least half full than you do when you are running on empty.

1. Feeling resentful, easily frustrated, or short-tempered much of the time.

2. Complaining of being tired.

3. Being overwhelmed.

4. Feeling isolated and alone.

5. Not feeling well physically frequently.

6. Having a negative attitude.

7. Overreacting to people and situations.

Do any of these sound familiar to you?

Keeping Water in Your Well

When I talk with moms about self-care, I find myself using the old adage about "keeping some water in the well." Are you feeling strong? Do you feel that you have within you what it takes to be a good mom? Are you feeling drained and depleted?

When I think about this old saying, I visualize a well that goes from my stomach to my heart. We all have a well within us. When I am taking care of myself, there is plenty of water in the well—plenty of patience and understanding and courage and love. When my well is full, I have plenty for myself, and plenty for others. When my well feels only half full, I know it's time to focus some time and energy on myself to refill it. If I don't have enough "water" for myself, I won't have enough for anyone else either.

Every mom has to find ways to fill her well. Depending on your life circumstances at the time, what can you do that will nourish you? As wonderful as it would be, few of us can jump on a plane and spend a week in Hawaii. We have to get much more creative and work with what we have.

When my youngest daughter, Carrie, was ten months old, she became very ill. I rocked her around the clock for several weeks. It was during this time that I learned many ways to feed my soul without being able to leave the house. I had no choice.

Here are some of the things I learned to do to make myself feel a little better each day. When I felt better, I could continue to give my baby and the rest of my family what they needed during those weeks.

Ask for help when you need it. I had no choice but to let friends bring meals, take my kids to school, do laundry. While it was hard for me to receive, I soon learned that they felt good about doing something that helped Baby Carrie and me. I had one friend whom Carrie would let hold her. She came everyday at 4:10 after work. She rocked her for an hour. During that time, I could do whatever I needed to put a little water in my well. Usually, it was something simple, like taking a shower or brushing my teeth. These simple things really made a difference for me. Sometimes, I just walked outside and stood in the sun. As Carrie's health improved, I even occasionally took a quick walk. It all helped. The accumulation of simple things throughout my day is what kept me going.

Bring some beauty into your house. Some days, I lit a candle and put it where I could see it as we rocked. Even a few fresh flowers on the table made me feel better.

Be accepting. Every day, I practiced acceptance. Accepting that my child was ill and that it was a challenging time for our family was not easy. But, in truth, there wasn't a better option. At that moment, my job was to rock my baby in my arms. I thought it, said it, wrote it, prayed it. I often wonder how many times I must have said the Serenity Prayer during those weeks.

Pray and meditate. Prayer and meditation became a frequent part of my day. The prayers kept me going. Friends and family were praying for us. Some friends came and prayed with me. I visualized my daughter being the picture of health once again, happily playing in the backyard.

Let go of the small stuff. I had no choice but to let go of things like my house always looking the way I liked it to. Dinners were healthy but simple. It was the Christmas season. I think we had a tree, but the rest of the decorations remained in their boxes that year. I followed Dolores Guetebier's advice to, "Ignore those dishes and watch your favorite movie instead, or just sit on your porch instead of scrubbing your floor. Give yourself permission to enjoy the crickets outside or the company of your family. Worry less about appearances and be in the moment!" *(Her Point of View)*

Breathe, breathe, breathe! Once again, I emphasize the importance of breathing. It's always with us. It doesn't cost anything. You can do it wherever you are. Whenever I felt myself getting tight, I simply took about ten deep breaths. The amazing thing was that, as I calmed from the breathing, so did Carrie.

Listen to music. I kept the TV off. Instead, I played calming and inspirational music most of the day. Sometimes, just singing along softly strengthened me. Other times, I put on happy children's music that lifted our spirits.

Receive only positive attitudes. I protected myself and my baby from anyone who was negative or fearful about the situation. There were so many loving and positive friends that showered us with all of the good thoughts and hopes that we needed.

Express gratitude. I had so much to be grateful for. I made sure that, many times each day, I acknowledged these blessings. At times, I was overwhelmed with the love and support that was showered on us. We were so blessed that we lived near one of the best hospitals and had the best doctors. We were blessed that the experimental medication appeared to be working, and that we lived in a small community that rallied to walk with us in Carrie's healing process.

Use humor. I have to admit I was exhausted. Much of the time, I didn't feel very humorous or want to laugh. However, every time someone did bring me some of their humor and laughter, I welcomed it. Laughter is cathartic. It's healing. Thank heavens I have a few friends who came often and always brought their humor with them! We all felt better after a good laugh!

These are just some of the ways that I discovered and found helpful during this particular time. There are many more that may help you keep water in your own well. Oh! And I imagine you may be wondering if the baby was okay. Moms do that sort of thing. Yes, she is grown up and is the picture of beauty and health today.

Finding Balance

Finding a balance that works for you and your children is a challenge for most of us. (That's an understatement!) What works and what is needed change over time as your family grows. How you do what you do makes the difference for you and your family. The more you create balance within your own life, the more your family as a whole benefits.

Balance is one of the foundation stones for taking care of yourself. Most moms are desperately searching for ways to find that balance in their busy lives. Sometimes, it feels nearly impossible to find a way to meet the endless demands of your family and somehow still find something that will keep water in your well. The ongoing question seems to be: How can I fit a thirty-six-hour day into twenty-four hours?

Lisa Hammond, author of *Dream Big* and *Stepping Stones,* says, "Balancing life is like standing on a balance beam. You must keep adjusting your body to find the center and then readjust to find it again and again."

I do know and understand the challenge. I lived with it for many years and still have to work to maintain the balance in my life. For me, the answer is simple—not so easy, but simple. *Simplify, simplify, simplify!* "How do I do that?" you ask.

You begin by looking at how you spend your days and the hours within each day. Prioritize what is most important. What are the areas that can be put on hold until your kids are a little older or your schedule opens up? Sometimes it's helpful to make a list of all your responsibilities and tasks. Trust me, it will be overwhelming. It will also give a good visual of just how much you are trying to do as a mom. There will be many things that you cannot eliminate. Fortunately, there are usually at least a few that you can either delegate to someone else, or simply decline to do at this time.

Go back and look at chapter 7. What are your golf balls? Your pebbles? Your sand? Eliminating the sand will help you simplify your life in more ways than you imagine. As you let go of the sand, you will discover, not only time in your day, but also extra energy.

Getting organized

When we become moms, we become what I call "organizational managers." Once you have simplified what you can in your life, it is easier to organize your day. Doing things like clumping your errands that are in the same part of town and doing them, if possible, without the kids saves you time. If you do need to take the kids, go at a time of day when they are rested and not hungry. If you have lots of errands to do, bring snacks. After two or three errands, stop at a park and let your kids run around and play for fifteen minutes and have a snack. Then finish up the errands.

Organize your meals. Many moms make a couple of dishes on the weekend and then eat off of them during the week. For example, if you cook a chicken for one night, you can have chicken tacos the next. Simplify.

As your kids grow to school age, get them involved in daily chores. You are not the butler or the maid. Earlier in the book, we talked about how giving children age-appropriate tasks not only keeps the household running more smoothly, it teaches them responsibility. It also teaches them that everyone in the family helps out. It's part of being a family.

Here's a conversation that took place in a parenting group. See if it rings a bell for you:

"All I do is laundry," says Ann, mom of twelve-, fourteen-, and seventeen-year-olds. "It's never caught up. Piles everywhere. The kids are always yelling at me because a certain shirt isn't clean the day they want it."

"Who's doing the laundry for your kids?" I ask.

"I am, of course. It's my job," she replies.

I take a deep breath and say, "Ann, somewhere along the way you got convinced that it's your job because you're the mom. However, your kids are old enough that each of them could be doing their own laundry quite capably." The room quieted. I could feel other moms thinking, "Really?"

"You've got to be kidding," Ann gasped. "They won't do it."

"Well, once you make them aware of the expectation and show them how to use the washer and dryer, it becomes their responsibility. If they choose not to do their laundry, then they will most likely have a couple of frustrating experiences when something isn't clean when they want it. But, in a short amount of time," I assured her, "they will take charge of making sure that they get their clothes washed ahead of time. This is one of those examples about setting a clear, age-appropriate limit with a natural and logical consequence. What would you say to them?"

Ann thought for a minute and said, "I would tell them that from now on, we'd all be responsible for our own laundry. I'd say, 'I will show you how to use the washer and dryer on Saturday. If you choose not to do your laundry, then your clothes will not be clean when you need them.' They are going to be so mad," she concluded.

"They may grumble at first," I acknowledged. "But in no time, they will be doing their laundry and actually feeling good about themselves. It will teach them responsibility as well as taking care of themselves. And it will help the family as a whole. Ann, you will be pleasantly surprised."

At the next class, Ann shared, "It worked! The two youngest got right into it. The oldest resisted, but came around when, one morning, he had baseball practice and his uniform was filthy from the last game. His coach lectured him for showing up in a dirty uniform. From there on out, he too began doing his laundry. You cannot imagine how much easier it is for me now."

Think of the areas where you are well-organized. Where would you like to be more organized? Talk with friends that seem to be organized in the areas where you need help. We can all learn so much from one another.

Planning ahead is part of being organized. If you are going to pick the kids up from school and have to go straight to an activity, bring some water and a healthy snack for them to have while you drive. They are stressed and tired from their day. Something healthy will help them be in a more cooperative mood.

If you are going somewhere that is unfamiliar to your children, talk with them ahead of time. Let them know where you're going, who will be there, and what you expect of them. Remember, your children do want to please you and have your approval. The more you let them know your expectations, the more cooperation you will most likely receive.

If your mornings are chaotic, try packing lunches the night before. Have the kids lay their clothes out for the next morning. Anything that you can do to simplify the morning will help. I used to have one of my children set the table for breakfast right after dinner. It sounds silly, but it only took a couple of minutes and, the next morning, the bowls, cereal, and utensils were already there. All we had to do was put out the milk and juice. It worked well for the kids and for me.

saying no

Many times, you may agree to give your time to help at school, with the soccer team, or at the church even though you know it's not a good idea right then. You know you are going to get too stressed.

Your family will end up losing out because you will be overtired and running on empty. It's great when you really do have the time and energy. However, for most moms who are working, managing the house, and being mom, there isn't much, if any, time left for other things.

Learning to say "No" takes practice. It takes courage. Your children have no problem with the word. Maybe you can look to them as teachers in this area. If you don't let your ego get in the way, there truly are some very valuable lessons that you can learn from children. Watch how easy it is for them to say no.

"No, I didn't get my homework done. I was too tired and fell asleep."

"Thank you for asking, but I won't be able to come over today."

"No, I don't care for lamb. I'll have salad."

They are clear with what they are willing to do and not do. They are not being disrespectful. They are simply making their limits known.

When I first realized that I simply had to learn to say no, it was extremely difficult. I didn't want to let anyone down. I was afraid that, if I didn't volunteer for something at the school, no one else would do it. The kids would lose out. As I showed earlier in the book, if you spread yourself too thin, that is when your children actually lose out.

I made myself a sign that read, "Just Say No!" I put a copy above the telephone, by the front door, and in my car. When someone called and asked me if I could give some of my time, I saw the sign. It was my reminder that my plate was already too full.

Initially, it was too hard to say, "No, I'm sorry, I won't be able to do that." So I started with saying something like, "Let me check my calendar and think about it. I'll get back to you." After doing this only three times, I realized it was more uncomfortable to call the person back and say no than it was to just say no in the first conversation.

I learned that, even if I couldn't do something at any given time, someone else could. The world didn't fall apart because I took care of myself and said no. I also realized that people accepted and respected my clear answer. It gave them permission to begin saying no when they needed to.

During this time in my life, a very wise friend of mine helped me to see that I didn't even have to give a reason. I simply needed to state clearly that I wouldn't be able to do what they were asking. I could not believe how people just accepted it. What freedom!

These three simple words can actually be another piece of Refrigerator Wisdom for you:

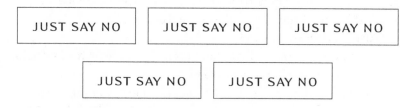

Taking care of yourself

One of my favorite sayings is: *You can't give what you don't have.* It's so true. As a mom, you need to be able to give to your children. You need to learn how to keep enough water in your well to care for yourself, your children, and other important people and events in your life. I am not saying that this is easy. It's not. I am saying it is vitally important to the well-being of you and your family.

There was a time in my life when my own well went dry. I became physically ill. My internal resources were depleted. My physical body was exhausted. It took nearly a year to heal. It was a very humbling and life-changing lesson. I learned the hard way just how vital it is to always keep some water in your well. Ever since then, I don't ever let the reserves in my well get low. In fact, I am so much happier and healthier when I keep it nearly full. It has become a way of life—taking care of myself.

Is it selfish to think this way? No. In order to give to your children or anyone else, you have to have something to give. Taking care of you is not selfish. It is a very wise and healthy thing to do. It benefits you and all those around you. When you take care of yourself, you take responsibility for yourself and your life. There is nothing selfish about that.

Jackie shared, "As a child, my parents always told me never to be selfish. To always share with my siblings. It's hard for me now not to feel selfish when I take some time for me. Today, for the first time, I think I'm getting it. There's a difference between being selfish in taking care of me and selfishness."

Others nodded. The light was dawning.

I also want to remind you that, even if you are feeling selfish, the bottom line is that, if you are not taking care of yourself, you cannot be the person you want to be. The more you take care of yourself and your needs, the more you will be there for others. The more you will have within you to contribute to your world. And the more you contribute, the more you become the person you are truly meant to be.

I want to acknowledge that every single day that you are in your recovery, you are taking care of you!

Here's a short list of what many moms do to take care of themselves. Take the ones you like and leave the rest for someone else. You can add more to the list.

1. Call my sponsor or a friend.

2. Go to a meeting.

3. Exercise.

4. Spend time with a friend over coffee or lunch.

5. Take a bubble bath.

6. Go to a movie.

7. Journal.

8. Read.

9. Watch a movie.

10. Go to the ocean or anywhere in nature.

11. Treat yourself to a manicure or pedicure.

12. Take a nap.

13. Listen to music.

Many times, it isn't possible to find ways to care for yourself without your children present. But you can do it even with your children there. You just need to be a little more creative. Here are some things you can do that may help both you and your children feel better.

Take a bike ride, a walk, a hike. You can enjoy the benefit of getting some exercise. Your children will enjoy not only the outside activity and what they may see along the way, but also the fact that they are spending time with you. We all benefit from being in nature.

Create artwork. Get some sheets of paper, crayons, paints, felt-tip pens, play-doh, clay, whatever you have. As your child creates a fun project, you can also tap into your creativity. By being creative, both moms and children can work through stressors and problems in ways that they don't even consciously realize.

Explore books and music. See if you can find some music or a book that both of you enjoy. With older children, it's fun to find a chapter book and spend time reading together every day. It's relaxing and, at the same time, helps you stay connected to your child.

Play games. Again, depending on the age of your children, find some games that you will all enjoy. There are many family-oriented, noncompetitive games today that can help build verbal communication. No one wins or loses. The purpose of the game is to have fun and connect.

Go to the park or the ocean. While your children play, you can have some quiet time just watching them, time to relax and enjoy nature. Throw in a snack that you all like. Sometimes, bringing some bubbles, a kite, a Frisbee, or a ball is fun. You may enjoy flying a kite or blowing bubbles more than you realize.

Make playdates. Invite another mom and her children to join you in an activity that you think you will all enjoy. For most moms, it is a gift when you are able to chat with another mom while watching the kids play.

Modeling Self-Respect

Be careful of the messages you are sending your children when you don't take care of yourself. When you neglect yourself, your children may think that you do not care for or value yourself. You send the message that you are not important.

It all comes down to love of self and self-respect. If you do not take care of yourself, you most likely do not yet love and respect yourself very much. Your children need you to model self-respect in order for them to learn to take care of themselves.

When you do take care of yourself, you send the message that you are an important and worthwhile person. You deserve to have some time to do things that help you to feel better about yourself, your children, and your family. You model that it's important to learn what fills a person's well and then to follow through on doing it. You also show your children that you want to be a good mom. When you take care of yourself, you are more equipped to be the mom you want to be—the mom your children deserve.

"It has been very hard for me to allow myself to do anything for me," said one mom. "I still have so much guilt about the mom I was before recovery. I know it's important though."

"For me, remaining in recovery is the most important thing," another mom said. "As long as I do that and continue with my sponsor, I am taking care of me."

Another shared this: "My kids know that, when I don't exercise, I get frustrated really easily. Sometimes, they will say, 'Mom, get your shoes and take a run.' When I do, I know I am doing all of us a favor. I come home with a better attitude."

And this mom acknowledged the importance of asking for help: "I am a single mom with four kids. I don't have a helpful family. Usually, the best I can do is breathe and pray, over and over. I do have friends that I could ask to take the kids once in awhile. That's what I need to work on: asking for help when I need it."

Jordan, age sixteen, told me, "My mom comes home tired from work. On a good day, we don't start fighting. We give her a little while to just change her clothes before she starts dinner. It doesn't sound like much, but she says it is helpful to her when she can take even fifteen to twenty minutes to regroup after a long workday."

Kyle added, "I can tell from my mom's face when her well is heading toward empty. She looks mad and acts as if we kids did something wrong all the time. Nothing is right. If she goes in her room and takes a shower and a nap, things usually get better. When I know she is trying to do something to help herself, I am more cooperative. When she refuses to do anything to get into a better mood, I get in a bad mood too."

Tomorrow Is a New Day

Every day is a new day. You can start over every day—first thing in the morning or, if need be, throughout the day.

Louise Hay, author of *You Can Heal Your Life,* says, "When I awaken, I spend about ten minutes thinking about all the good in my life. I then program my day, affirming that everything will go well and that I will enjoy it." Sometimes, however, while you may have had Louise's intention, your day becomes just the opposite—obstacle after obstacle. At these times, dig a little deeper and ask for what you need, whether it be strength, clarity, or patience. I know it is hard, but learning to be gentle and kind with yourself is so important.

Mary Anne Radmacher, author of *Courage Doesn't Always Roar,* says:

> Courage does not always roar,
> sometimes it's that quiet voice,
> at the end of the day that says,
> "I will try again tomorrow."

Can you hear the kindness to herself in those words, as well as her intention to try again tomorrow?

JOURNALING ACTIVITY

1. Make a list of the things that you may allow to get in the way of your self-care.

2. How do you know when the water in your well is low?

3. Make a list of all of the things that you can do to take care of yourself.

4. What can you and your children do together that will nurture all of you?

5. Make any Refrigerator Wisdom signs that may be helpful. For example, "Breathe!" "Just Say NO!" "Take time for me," "I am important too."

GEMS FOR YOUR POCKET

"If mama ain't happy, ain't nobody happy." Do what you need to do to lighten up.

Your mood affects your children's moods.

It is important to take good care of yourself. You are worth it.

Keep some water in your well.

Prioritize and let go of anything you can that takes your time and energy.

Find ways to become more organized.

Plan ahead.

Let your children know what you expect of them.

Learn to say "No" when appropriate.

Ask for help when you need it. Remember, the person giving the help is also receiving a gift—the good feeling we get when we help someone else.

You deserve to take some time to do something that will help you feel better about yourself and rejuvenate you for another day.

AFFIRMATIONS

I am a valuable and important person.

I consistently take good care of myself.

I am worthwhile.

I love myself.

I know what I need. I take care of my needs.

I am healthy and strong.

I find ways to give myself some time just for me.

I am well organized.

I simplify my life wherever I can.

I ask for help when I need it.

I am strong in my recovery.

I am enough.

continuing your journey

Go confidently in the direction of your dreams.
Live the life you've imagined.

—Henry David Thoreau

Every mom wants to succeed—to create the life that, maybe up until now, you thought was impossible. Remaining strong in your recovery, finishing your education, having a job you enjoy, and providing a secure and safe place to call home are all within your reach. What does the life you want look like? Continue to move forward on your path. *You have within you what it takes to make your dreams a reality.*

Having a caring and supportive community is important for moms and their children. We all want positive role models, encouragement, and support. Moms value other moms. You have a connection because you share an understanding of what it is like to be a mom in recovery, working so hard to create a good life for you and your children.

I understand that, for some of you, it may feel nearly impossible to allow yourself to dream about the life you want. From deep within my heart, I encourage you to nudge yourself in that direction. You are as deserving as every other person on the face of this Earth.

A group of twelve- to fourteen-year-olds created this list of what every child wants in a mom.

1. She remains in her recovery.

2. She is trustworthy.

3. She is there for us in good times and bad.

4. She keeps us safe and secure. She protects us.

5. She makes sure there is food in the refrigerator. Pizza on Fridays.

6. She gets us new school clothes and shoes.

7. She doesn't embarrass us.

8. She does what she says she will do.

9. She doesn't abuse us in any way.

10. She is funny sometimes.

11. She takes us to the doctor when we need to go.

12. She likes us.

13. She doesn't put us down.

14. She encourages us to get a good education.

15. She tells us we are great!

They also made a list of what they want for themselves:

1. To have fun.

2. To be happy.

3. To be a good person.

4. To be healthy and strong.

5. To have good friends.

6. To go to college.

7. To accomplish our goals.

8. To feel good about ourselves.

9. To love and trust our moms and families.

10. To be proud of ourselves.

11. To have self-respect.

12. To have nice clothes.

13. To be able to go places.

14. To feel like I belong to a "village."

Erik, age thirteen, said, "I want to be the first one in my family to go to college and graduate. My mom says if I keep getting good grades, we will figure out how to make it happen. I believe her. She didn't get to go to college, but she sure wants for us kids to be able to. She says it will help make parts of our lives easier someday. I know she is proud of me."

Ashley shared, "I just want to have clothes like other girls. I want to fit in, to feel like I am one of the group. Before my mom was in recovery, she didn't care what I had for clothes. It was pretty embarrassing."

Jacob, age fourteen, moved here two years ago from Oregon. He shared, "I had been away from my mom for three years when the judge finally gave me back to her. She was so happy. It was hard for me to come here and not know anyone. I had family, friends, and a church up in Oregon. I was pretty mad when I first got here, because I felt like I didn't fit in anywhere and I didn't even know my mom. I was so mad at her for getting me back. I got into a lot of trouble at school and the mall at first. It took a year, but now I feel like I did when I was in Oregon. I have friends and family here too. My mom's church has a youth group that has helped a lot. The church is our village. They have helped my mom and me in many ways. Once I saw that my mom was different now that she was sober, I quit being so mean to her. But it still took me quite a while to forgive her and begin to trust her. She didn't let me abuse her, but she did give me time and space to work my stuff through."

Looking Back so you can Move Forward

Some of you had parents who were addicts. Some of them chose recovery and some did not. They may not have had dreams for their lives or for you. Their journeys did not look like the one you have chosen.

Kathy shared, "My parents would have laughed anyone right out of the bar if they had asked them what they hoped for themselves. For their children. My dad would have said he hoped the booze would never run out. For his kids, he hoped they would leave home before they got themselves pregnant or in trouble. He thought it was all very funny. He had no real hope or ambition. Until my recovery, I had never been around anyone who had hopes and dreams for their life. I thought all adults were like my parents. Now I know there are a lot of people who are honest, kind, and responsible."

Erin confided, "My mom was always telling us that, soon, our dad would come back. We would buy a big house and have everything we wanted. I believed her for many years. A part of me, even as a teen, didn't want to give up the fantasy. Of course, it never happened. None of it. I would have been so much better off if she had told us the truth. I still have resentment for her because of the lies all those years. Maybe a part of her really believed he'd be back. She never really got on with her life. She just waited for him to come and fix everything. It's really pretty sad to see the results of the choices she's made."

Shelley said, "My mom was a single mom, but she had an education. She was a nurse. So while we never had a lot of money, we had the basics. She always told me that, if I wanted to go to college, she would find a way. She told me life is hard without an education. My grandfather told me just the opposite—that I wasn't smart enough to go to college and that my mom would never have the money anyway. Unfortunately, I listened to him rather than my mom. I found myself homeless and addicted. I wish I had listened to her rather than him. My life might have been different. I still may get back to college one of these days."

"We moved so often I don't ever remember feeling like we had any kind of a community," Anna shared. "It was pretty much just my mom and us kids. I think I went to seven different schools. I had a hard time making friends. I think it was because I knew we would move soon. I didn't want to get close to anyone."

Juanita piped in, "My family is huge. I don't even know all of my relatives. I guess that would be my community. There was always lots of partying on weekends. All of us kids just hung out while our parents got drunk. None of them are in my life now. I miss them, but it doesn't work for me to have them in my life. I am building my own village, family by family. We help one another, especially with child care and rides."

Therese added, "My parents were very religious. We were at the church two to three times every week. That was our family, our village. Everything we did was with the families who belonged to the same church. I hated going there, but I liked all of the extra things we did, like family campouts, potlucks, Christmas caroling.

You may think it sounds dorky, but I felt like I had a big family in those days. I liked it. I wish I had one now for me and my kids."

Now that you have chosen recovery, opportunities for the life you want are opening. You are a woman of courage and perseverance. Whether you know it or not, *you can be anything you want to be.* It doesn't matter how young or old you are, how much money you have in your bank account, or how long you have been in recovery. The more you continue to release fear and doubt about yourself, the more you forgive yourself and others for the past, the more you will move forward in your life.

Here's another piece of Refrigerator Wisdom for you, written by Mary Anne Radmacher.

all i know is this . . .
you can get there
from here.
you can walk through the
fear.
travel past what is gone before.
wake up!
wake up and get up on the other side.
dare to become that of
your dreams.
dare!
dare to believe in your own possibility.

Mary Anne pretty well covers it in this quote from her signature poster collection, which can be found at *maryanneradmacher.com.*

setting short-term goals

Your life is like a road map. There are many roads, curves, stop signs, mountaintops, and valleys. You can decide which road to take. As of this very moment, you can choose to go in any direction. I don't mean literally traveling. I mean making decisions that will head you in a direction that will let you manifest the life you want.

Your recovery is your main road. It's your superhighway. But there are many different side roads to choose from that still keep you on the highway and allow you to create your life. Once you set your goals, you can begin heading in that direction one step at a time.

Here's what some moms say about the journey:

> "My job is important, but right now my real goal is to make our house feel more like a home."

> "I've been taking classes at the college for a couple of years. It seems like it's taking forever. But every time I get my grades, I am so proud and know that I am getting closer to my AA degree."

> "I am concentrating on my health right now. My doctor and I have a plan. It helps that she is guiding and supporting me."

These moms have all chosen realistic goals for themselves. Once your goal is set, you have to map out the steps you'll need to take to get there.

One mom set the goal of creating "home" for her family. Her first step might be to figure out what she wants the house to look like when she is finished. Go ahead. Imagine it. Visualize it. Once she can see it in her head, she can begin making a list of what needs to be done. Then she can look at the list and decide what needs to be done first, and next, and so on. She can also figure out how much it is going to cost her for each step. She knows how much she makes, so she can figure out how much she can put away or spend toward the project from each paycheck.

The process takes time. Acknowledge yourself for accomplishing each step you take. Enjoy the process!

Here is an example from a woman named Maggie who had two young children and was getting ready to move into a two-bedroom unfurnished apartment. Her goal was to furnish the apartment for her kids and herself.

STEP 1: Make a list of everything we already have.

STEP 2: Make a list of everything we are going to need.

STEP 3: Check the items that are most important to get first.

STEP 4: Looking at step 3, figure out how much each item will cost individually, and how much it will probably cost altogether.

STEP 5: Make a list of places to get the needed items.

STEP 6: Make a list of friends who said they might have some extra things for her.

STEP 7: Make those phone calls.

Sure enough, many of the items from the list in Step 3 were available from friends who were happy to pass them on to her. By the time Maggie got to Step 3, she was so excited. She felt proud of what she was accomplishing. By the time she got to Step 7, she knew that she really was creating the home she had set out to create. She felt very proud of herself and the way in which she was proceeding. Maggie kept referring back to her list and noting what was taken care of and what still needed to be addressed. She continued one step at a time. When moving day came, she had the basics and more to begin life in her family's new home!

While it is important to live in the moment for many aspects of your life, it is also important to take responsibility for your needs and wants down the road. If Maggie had not planned ahead, moving day would have come and I don't think she would have felt as if she were creating the home she wanted. I think she would have been very stressed and overwhelmed because she wasn't prepared and organized.

As I said in chapter 10, when you become a mom, you become an organizational manager. When you plan things out ahead of time, there is less chaos and confusion. If you are less stressed, your children are likely to be less stressed as well.

Here are some more tips on learning to be organized:

Make lists: Write down what needs to be done today, tomorrow, and so on. Start a grocery list. When it's time to do the weekly shopping, you'll have it ready.

Keep a calendar: In the kitchen where everyone in the family can see it, keep track of schedules. Doctor's appointments, soccer games, birthday parties, you name it—it goes on the calendar. Get into the habit of glancing at it during the day. Take another look before you go to bed and see what's on the schedule for tomorrow. Sometimes, it helps to be reminded that tomorrow is, for example, picture day at school. Then you can put a load of wash in and make sure that the clothes will be clean for the pictures. This can eliminate yelling and tears in the morning.

Find a place for things: Let everyone know where everything goes, and they can easily be put away. If you have too much "stuff," get rid of what you don't need. If your kids have clothes they've outgrown, pass them on to someone who can use them or donate them to a thrift shop. Involve your children in deciding what needs to be passed on and what you're going to do with it. It's a great way to involve them in learning to help others. It will be much easier for you and your children to keep things organized once you recycle the things you no longer need and find a place for the ones you plan to keep.

Manifesting Your Dreams

Take some time now and then to think about and imagine how you want your life to be in five years. If you are someone who enjoys writing, write about it. Date it. You may be very surprised, when you come across it five years from now, that you have brought all of your dreams into your life.

Recently, I was talking with a friend who has been in recovery for many years about manifesting her dreams. She was a little confused about what I meant. I pulled out a list of things that I had written five or six years before that I wanted to create in my life. Out of the thirty-four items on the list, all but three had come into my life! Even I was surprised! Get together with some friends or your sponsor and share your dreams. Dream big!

When asked about her big dreams, Bonnie began, "That's easy for me. I have always wanted to travel. Anywhere. I'd like to go to a country and work with children; maybe children who have AIDS. I want to do something like that. Something that will make a difference."

"I want to have a happy and solid marriage and two kids," said Liz. "I want to be able to give them the good things in life. Not spoil them. But to have more than I ever did."

Alyssa commented, "I want my own horse." Everyone chuckled. She went on to say that all her life she had wanted a horse, a beautiful one. "And I want to learn to be a really good rider."

Here are some other comments from the group:

"I want to be a high school teacher. I want to influence teens to make better choices than I did."

"I want to heal with my mom and brothers."

"I want to be in a triathlon."

"I want to be a well-known and really good musician."

"I want to be the first one of my family to graduate from college. I can see myself walking across the stage already. I also want all four of my kids to do the same."

Then we talked about all the things that can get in the way of realizing our big dreams. Here's what these moms said:

"What else . . . fear. It stops everything."

"I'm chicken to try anything. I guess that's fear."

"Takes money and I never have any."

"I'm a slow reader. How could I ever get through the classes?"

The list of excuses could have gone on and on. But when we really looked at them, we saw two common themes: fear and attitude.

Ever heard the saying: "Feel the fear and do it anyway?" If need be, go back and read the parts of this book where we talked about fear. If you are feeling afraid or negative about things, maybe your Gremlin has returned—you know, that voice of negative judgment. Tell it firmly to go elsewhere. You have no room or time for ol' Gremlin any longer.

In one class, moms found it was much easier to share the dreams they had for their children than the dreams they had for themselves.

"That they won't ever get into drugs."

"That they will go to college."

"That she'll find a man who will treat her well."

"That he'll be happy and healthy. He'll like who he is."

"That she'll be a better mom than I was to her."

And when I asked the children, here's what they said:

"I want to get good grades and go to college."

"I want to have a family and be a good mom."

"I want to be an artist."

"I want my family to get along."

"I want to know that I am a good person."

The key to making these dreams come true is to acknowledge them and make a plan. I have used these three questions to help me reach both the big and the small goals that I have set in my life:

What do I want?

What do I need to do to get it?

When do I want it?

Here's an example of how these three simple questions can help you fulfill a small dream:

I want to go to the ocean for a day.

I need to ask for the day off; I need to put gas in the car; I need to bring a jacket, a blanket, and my journal.

I want to go in the next ten days.

I am clear on what I want and what I have to do to accomplish it. The reason for setting a time for completion is that, if you don't have some kind of target time or date, you may very well end up procrastinating and putting it off. And then it never comes to be. If, for some reason, you say you want to go within the next ten days and it turns out you can't go for three weeks, that's okay. You don't need to beat yourself up. You just need to hold yourself accountable that you will go in three weeks. If it keeps happening and you don't follow through, then you need to figure out why you are not doing what you said you wanted to do. Are you being lazy? Are you sabotaging having something good come into your life? Do you believe that you don't deserve a day at the ocean?

Here's an example of something on a bigger scale:

I want to buy a house.

I need to find a good realtor; I need to talk to a bank to see what I can afford; I need to think about what kind of a house I want and decide on appropriate areas. Once I know how much I can afford, I can begin looking at places. I might need to get pre-approved. When I find what I want, I can work with the realtor to make an offer. I need to make sure I understand what the contract says.

My goal is to buy the house within the next one to three years.

I hope you can see how these three simple questions can help you to map out your goals, big or small.

Being HeLd AccountabLe

Sometimes, when you are setting a goal and are doing all you can to accomplish it, it helps to ask a trusted friend to hold you accountable. Tell them what you are planning to do and when you want it done. Ask if your friend will hold you accountable. If he or she agrees, you can also ask your friend to check in with you, or vice versa, on a specific day. Set it up so that you are both clear on the goal and the agreement. This is meant to support you in following through. For most of us, just having someone hold us accountable helps us to keep going at those times when, on our own, we might not.

If you do not achieve your goal, your friend is not going to send you on a guilt trip or shame you. It may be helpful for the two of you to talk about what got in the way. And then make another plan and go for it!

Hillary is the mom of four-year-old twins and a new baby. She had always read two books to the twins every night until the baby arrived. Now the bedtime routine was falling apart because the twins wanted their stories as usual, and Hillary was busy with the baby. When the baby was six weeks old, Hillary asked me to hold her accountable that she would get the baby to bed early enough to be able to read to the twins each night.

A part of me didn't think it was going to work. But she was not asking me for advice. She was asking me to hold her accountable. I agreed. She wanted to do it for four to five nights and then check in with me.

The morning after the second night, she called in tears. "Barbara, it's not working. I can't do it. I am just too tired by that time of night." It made perfect sense to me that, of course, she was exhausted by the end of the day. After a few minutes, we began talking about a way that it could work for all of them. She came up with another idea. "I will read them their books in the late afternoon while the baby naps," she said. "At bedtime, they can look at books while I get the baby to sleep. Then I will talk quietly with them a few minutes and tuck them in for the night." Once again, I agreed to hold her accountable with her new plan.

A few days later, a happier Hillary called. There had been initial grumbling from the twins about the change in their routine, but that was temporary. They loved their afternoon book time with their mom. Hillary was enjoying the reading time with the girls so much more because she was not quite so exhausted and wasn't distracted with the new baby. Hillary felt good about herself because she had come up with a plan that worked for her and her children.

You work hard in many areas of your life. I encourage you to begin celebrating every goal you reach. Big or small. Maybe you were patient for an afternoon with your kids. Maybe you finished the laundry. Maybe you took that walk you've been wanting to take or made that phone call. Maybe you've now been in your job for six months. Maybe you stopped doing the dishes and sat down and listened to your upset teen. It's all success. It's all important.

You find your way one step at a time. As you acknowledge each step and each goal met, you move forward to the next step, and then the next. With each step, your dreams come closer to becoming your reality.

ceLebrate yourseLf

As we come to the end of this book, I want to acknowledge you. I want to celebrate you. It may be redundant, but I want to say this one more time.

You are a strong and determined woman. I am continually touched that you have overcome many obstacles in order to be the person that you truly are. I admire your honesty and humility. I respect you for taking responsibility for your past and choosing recovery. You are succeeding in your life. Not only are you giving yourself the gift of you, you are giving it to your children and to the rest of the world. Your journey is important.

JOURNALING ACTIVITY

1. Make a list of short-term goals: for one month, for six months, for a year.

2. Write about your long-term goals.

3. Using my three questions, map out what you will need to do to accomplish these goals. Think about whom you can ask to hold you accountable when you are ready.

4. What are your dreams for your children?

5. Talk with your children and ask them what their dreams are for themselves. Write them in your journal. It will be fun to look back at them in a few years.

6. Write about ways to celebrate yourself and each accomplishment.

7. Take a little time and look back through this book. What has been most helpful to you? Most interesting to you? Write it down. Turn back to it when you need a little reminder or some encouragement.

8. Write a huge self-acknowledgment to yourself for finishing this book!

GEMS FOR YOUR POCKET

You have within you what it takes to make your dreams a reality.
Go ahead—dream big!

Create a supportive community.

Set short-term and long-term goals.

Acknowledge yourself for every single accomplishment,
big or small.

Feel the fear and do it anyway.

Ask a trusted friend to hold you accountable when you think
it will help you.

Nurture and enjoy yourself and your children.

Always remember that you are a woman of perseverance and
courage. You deserve to have a fulfilling life.

AFFIRMATIONS

I take one step at a time, striving to be the best mom I can be.

I set short-term goals and follow through.

I allow myself to dream big.

I am worthy of good things coming into my life.

I can do and be whatever I desire.

I am a strong and determined woman.

I am well-organized.

I plan ahead.

My home is safe and secure.

I am filled with self-confidence.

My children are filled with self-confidence.

I celebrate each accomplishment.

I am proud of myself and my children.

I am strong in my recovery.

I am enough.

Indeed, you are absolutely enough. May you continue on your journey with love and gratitude in your heart, as you create the very best life for you and your children.

Recommended Readings

ENCOURAGEMENT AND INSPIRATION

Beattie, Melody. *Codependent No More.* Center City, MN: Hazelden, 1992.

———. *The Language of Letting Go.* Center City, MN: Hazelden, 1990.

Black, Claudia. *It Will Never Happen to Me: Growing Up with Addiction as Youngsters, Adolescents, Adults.* Center City, MN: Hazelden, 2002.

Brown Stephanie, Ph.D. *Treating the Alcoholic.* San Francisco: Wiley, 1996.

Casey, Karen. *Change Your Mind and Your Life Will Follow.* San Francisco: Conari Press, 2007.

Covington, Stephanie, Ph.D. *A Woman's Way Through the Twelve Steps.* Center City, MN: Hazelden, 1994.

Cox, Meg. *The Heart of a Family: Searching America for New Traditions That Fulfill Us.* New York: Random House, 1998.

Ford, Judy. *Wonderful Ways to Be a Family.* San Francisco: Conari Press, 2006.

———. *Wonderful Ways to Love a Child.* San Francisco: Conari Press, 2003.

Gorski, Terrence. *Recovery from Addiction.* Independence, MO: Herald House Independence Press, 2008.

Hammond, Lisa. *Dream Big.* San Francisco: Conari Press, 2004.

———. *Stepping Stones.* San Francisco: Conari Press, 2005.

Hay, Louise. *You Can Heal Your Life.* Carlsbad, CA: Hay House, 1984.

Kenison, Katrina. *Mitten Strings for God: Reflections for Mothers in a Hurry.* Clayton, VIC: Warner Books, 2002.

Lafia, Colette. *Comfort and Joy: Simple Ways to Care for Ourselves and Others.* San Francisco: Conari Press, 2008.

Marston, Ralph S., Jr. *Awaken* and *Living the Wonder of It All.* Austin, TX: Image Express, Inc., 2004.

Nelsen, Jane. *Serenity: Simple Steps for Recovering Peace of Mind, Real Happiness, and Great Relationships.* San Francisco: Conari Press, 2008.

Radmacher, Mary Anne. *Courage Doesn't Always Roar.* San Francisco: Conari Press, 2009.

———. *Lean Forward into Your Life.* San Francisco: Conari Press, 2007.

———. *Live Boldly.* San Francisco: Conari Press, 2008.

Richardson, Cheryl. *Take Time for Your Life.* New York: Broadway Books, 1998.

Rogers, Barb. *Twenty-five Words.* San Francisco: Red Wheel, 2005.

Ruis, Don Miguel. *The Four Agreements.* San Francisco: Amber-Allen Publishing Inc., 1997.

Ryan, M. J. *Attitudes of Gratitude.* San Francisco: Conari Press, 2002.

Siegel, Bernie, MD. *Love, Magic, and Mudpies.* New York: Rodale, 2006.

PARENTING TOOLS AND EDUCATION

Ames, Louise Bates, Ph.D, and Carol Chase Haber, M.A. *Your One-Year-Old* through *Your Ten- to Fourteen-Year-Old.* New York: Dell Publishing, 1990.

Brazelton, T. Berry. *Touchpoints* (books and video series). New York: Da Capo Press, 1994.

Burt, Sandran, and Linda Perlis. *Raising a Successful Child.* Berkeley: Ulysses Press, 2006.

Faber, Adele, and Elaine Mazlish. *How to Talk So Your Kids Will Listen and Listen So Your Kids Will Talk.* New York: Avon Books, Inc., 1999.

———. *Siblings without Rivalry.* New York: Avon Books, 2004.

Glenn, Stephen, and Jane Nelsen. *Raising Self-Reliant Children in a Self-Indulgent World.* New York: Three Rivers Press, 2000.

Hartley-Brewer, Elizabeth. *Talking to Tweens.* New York: Da Capo Press, 2005.

Karp, Dr. Harry. *Happiest Baby on the Block* (book and video). New York: Bantam Books, 2003.

Kohn, Alfie. *Unconditional Parenting: Moving from Rewards and Punishment to Love and Reason.* New York: Atria Books, 2005.

MacKenzie, Robert. *Setting Limits.* New York: Three Rivers Press, 1998.

Nelsen, Jane, Riki Inter, and Lynn Lott. *Positive Discipline for Parenting in Recovery.* Available through *www.empoweringpeople.com.*

Samalin, Nancy. *Love and Anger: The Parental Dilemma.* New York: Penguin Books, 1991.

———. *Loving Your Child Is Not Enough.* New York: Penguin Books, 1998.

Siegel, Daniel, and Mary Hartzell. *Parenting from the Inside Out.* New York: Penguin, 2004.

popular parenting web sites

GENERAL PARENT EDUCATION

Melody Beattie
(Codependency and Inspiration)
www.melodybeattie.com

T. Berry Brazelton
(Emotional and Behavioral
Development)
www.touchpoints.org

Adele Faber and **Elaine Mazlish**
(Sibling Rivalry)
www.fabermazlish.com

Jane Nelsen
(Positive Discipline)
www.empoweringpeople.com
www.positivediscipline.com

Nancy Samalin
(Handling Anger and Discipline)
www.samalin.com

Bernie Siegel, MD
(Raising Happy, Healthy,
Loving Kids)
www.berniesiegelmd.com

ENCOURAGEMENT AND INSPIRATION

Karen Casey
www.womens-spirituality.com

Judy Ford
www.judyford.com

Ralph S. Marston, Jr.
www.DailyMotivator.com

Mary Anne Radmacher
www.maryanneradmacher.com

Cheryl Richardson
www.cherylrichardson.com

Mary Jane Ryan
www.mj-ryan.com

About the Author

Barbara Joy has been working with parents and children for more than thirty years as a coach, consultant, educator, nurse, and advocate. The last fifteen years have included work with parents in recovery and their children. She teaches and consults in both short- and long-term treatment centers and works individually with moms who have been in recovery for many years. Barbara is passionate about assisting parents in raising happier, healthier children thus creating happier, healthier families. She has three grown children and four grandchildren and lives in Santa Rosa, California. Visit her at *www.parentingwithjoy.com.*